ESTATE PU̶̶̶̶̶̶̶NS

DORSET

C000256086

Street maps with index
Administrative Districts
Population Gazetteer
Road Map with index
Postcode Districts

COUNTY RED BOOKS

This atlas is intended for those requiring street maps of the historical and commercial centres of towns within the county. Each locality is normally presented on one or two pages and although, with many small towns, this space is sufficient to portray the whole urban area, the maps of large towns and cities are for centres only and are not intended to be comprehensive. Such coverage is offered in the Super and Local Red Book (see page 2).

Street plans prepared and published by ESTATE PUBLICATIONS, Bridewell House, TENTERDEN, KENT, and based upon the ORDNANCE SURVEY mapping with the permission of The Controller of H. M. Stationery Office.

The publishers acknowledge the co-operation of the local authorities of towns represented in this atlas.

© Estate Publications 136 G   ISBN 0 86084 776 4   © Crown Copyright 398713

COUNTY RED BOOK

DORSET

contains street maps for each town centre

SUPER & LOCAL RED BOOKS

are street atlases with comprehensive local coverage

BOURNEMOUTH

including: Bransgore, Christchurch, Corfe Mullen, Ferndown, Milford-on-Sea, New Milton, Poole, Ringwood, Sway, Verwood, Wimborne Minster etc.

WEYMOUTH & DORCHESTER

including: Chickerell, Easton, Fortuneswell, Preston, Upwey etc.

CONTENTS

Scale of street plans: 4 inches to 1 mile (unless otherwise stated on map)

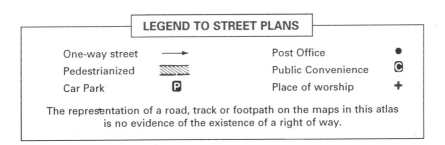

LEGEND TO STREET PLANS

One-way street	⟶	Post Office	●
Pedestrianized	▨	Public Convenience	Ⓒ
Car Park	Ⓟ	Place of worship	✦

The representation of a road, track or footpath on the maps in this atlas
is no evidence of the existence of a right of way.

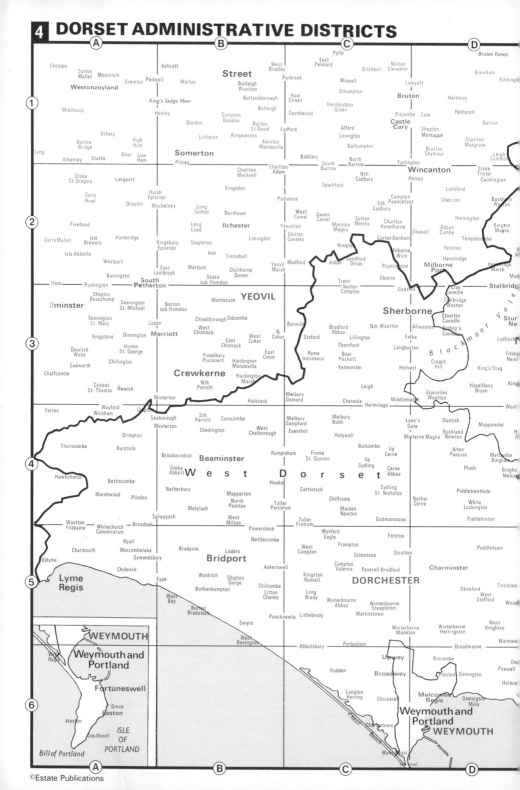

©Estate Publications

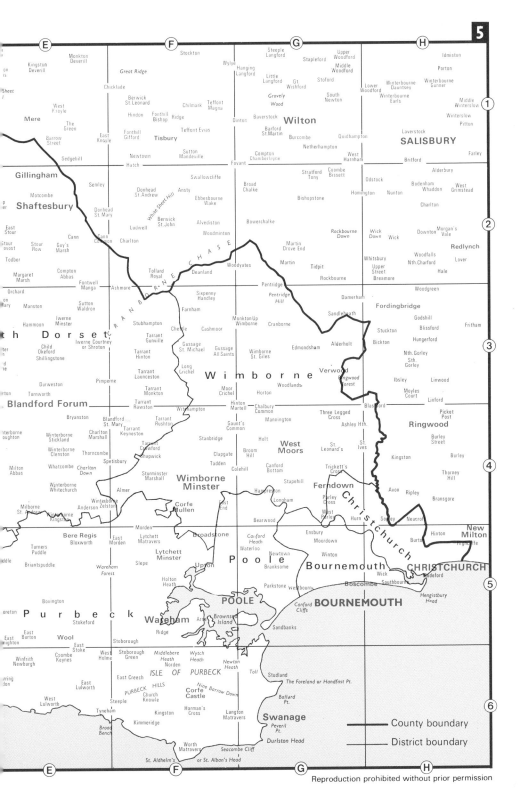

5

E F G H

County boundary
District boundary

GAZETTEER INDEX TO ROAD MAP
with Populations

County of Dorset population **645,166**

Districts:

Bournemouth	151,302
Christchurch	40,865
East Dorset	78,698
North Dorset	52,110
Poole	133,050
Purbeck	42,445
West Dorset	85,463
Weymouth & Portland	61,233

Abbotsbury **422**	11 E5
Adber	8 A3
Affpuddle **447**	12 A4
Alderholt **2,880**	9 H4
Allington **649**	*
Allweston	8 B4
Almer	12 C3
Alton Pancras **147**	11 G2
Anderson **71**	12 C3
Arne **1,154**	12 D5
Ashley Heath	13 F2
Ashmore **157**	9 E3
Askerswell **146**	10 D4
Athelhampton **48**	*
Batcombe **83**	11 F2
Beaminster **2,769**	10 D2
Bearwood	13 E3
Beer Hackett **99**	8 A4
Bere Regis **1,767**	12 B4
Bettiscombe **71**	10 B3
Bincombe **542**	11 G5
Bingham's Melcombe	12 A3
Bishop's Caundle **375**	8 B4
Blandford Forum **7,957**	12 C2
Blandford St Mary **923**	12 C2
Bloxworth **192**	12 B4
Boscombe	13 F4
Bothenhampton **1,823**	10 D4
Bournemouth **90,636**	13 F4
Bourton **675**	8 C1
Bovington	12 B4
Bradford Abbas **932**	8 A4
Bradford Peverell **348**	*
Bradpole **2,056**	10 D4
Branksome	13 E4
Briantspuddle	12 B4
Bridport **7,278**	10 D4
Broadmayne **1,134**	11 G5
Broakoak	10 C3
Broadstone **9,223**	12 D3
Broadwey	11 F5
Broadwindsor **1,223**	10 C2
Broom Hill	13 E2
Bryanston **382**	12 B2
Buckhorn Weston **355**	8 C2
Buckland Newton **551**	11 G2
Burleston **30**	12 A4
Burstock **110**	10 C2
Burton **4,086**	13 G4
Burton Bradstock **898**	10 D4
Canford Bottom	13 E4
Cann **477**	9 E2
Cann Common	9 E2
Cashmoor	9 F4
Castleton **157**	*
Catherston Leweston **64**	*

Cattistock **440**	11 E3
Caundle Marsh **59**	*
Cerne Abbas **661**	11 F3
Chalbury Common **163**	13 E2
Chaldon Herring or	
E. Chaldon **167**	12 A5
Charlestown	11 F6
Charlton Marshall **956**	12 C2
Charminster **1,615**	11 G4
Charmouth **1,138**	10 B4
Chedington **100**	10 D2
Cheselbourne **275**	12 A3
Chetnole **368**	11 E2
Chettle **69**	9 F4
Chickerell **4,217**	11 F6
Chideock **625**	10 C4
Chilcombe **11**	10 D4
Child Okeford **1,012**	8 D4
Chilfrome **46**	11 E3
Christchurch **31,086**	13 H4
Church Knowle **329**	12 C6
Clapgate	12 D2
Clifton Maybank **52**	*
Colehill **7,237**	12 D3
Compton Abbas **204**	9 E3
Compton Valence **52**	11 E4
Coombe Keynes **97**	12 B5
Corfe Castle **1,335**	12 D6
Corfe Mullen **9,804**	12 D3
Corscombe **470**	10 D2
Cranborne **667**	9 G4
Crossways **1,745**	12 A5
Crouch Hill	8 B4
Deanland	9 F3
Dewlish **235**	12 A3
Dorchester **15,037**	11 F4
Drimpton	10 C2
Duntish	11 G2
Durweston **305**	8 D4
East Burton	12 B5
East Chelborough **49**	*
East Creech	12 C5
East End	12 D3
East Holme **59**	*
East Knighton	12 A5
East Lulworth **188**	12 B6
East Morden	12 C4
Easton (with	
Fortuneswell) **12,742**	10 B6
East Orchard **103**	8 D3
East Stoke **460**	12 B5
East Stour **467**	8 D2
Edmondsham **205**	9 G4
Ensbury **7,911**	13 E3
Evershot **225**	11 E2
Eype	10 C4
Farnham **207**	9 F3
Ferndown **16,294**	13 E3
Fifehead Magdalen **81**	8 C3
Fifehead Neville **119**	8 C4
Fleet **90**	*
Folke **327**	8 B4
Fontmell Magna **569**	9 E3
Forston	11 F3
Fortuneswell (with	
Easton) **12,742**	10 B6

Frampton **405**	11 F4
Frome St Quintin **158**	11 E2
Frome Vauchurch **161**	*
Gaunt's Common	12 D2
Gillingham **6,934**	8 D2
Glanvilles Wootton **183**	11 F1
Goathill **18**	8 B3
Godmanstone **131**	11 F3
Grimstone	11 F4
Grove	10 B6
Gussage All Saints **215**	9 G4
Gussage St Michael **203**	9 F4
Guy's Marsh	8 D3
Halstock **339**	10 D2
Hammoon **36**	8 D4
Hamworthy **12,125**	12 D4
Hanford **36**	*
Harman's Cross	12 D6
Haydon **32**	*
Hazelbury Bryan **700**	8 C4
Hermitage **104**	11 F2
Highcliffe	13 G4
Higher Ansty	12 A2
Hilfield **70**	*
Hilton **451**	12 A2
Hinton Martell **385**	12 D2
Hinton Parva **50**	*
Hinton St Mary **203**	8 D3
Holnest **185**	8 B4
Holt **1,261**	13 E2
Holton Heath	12 C4
Holworth	12 A5
Holywell **393**	11 E2
Hooke **112**	10 B3
Horton **574**	13 E2
Hurn **400**	13 F3
Ibberton **120**	12 A2
Iwerne Courtney	
or Shroton **384**	9 E4
Iwerne Minster **584**	8 D4
Iwerne Stepleton **27**	*
Kimmeridge **94**	12 C6
King's Stag	8 C4
Kingston	8 C4
Kingston (Purbeck)	12 D6
Kingston Russell **48**	11 E4
Kington Magna **364**	8 C2
Knap Corner	8 D2
Langton Herring **151**	11 F6
Langton Long Blandford **118**	*
Langton Matravers **910**	12 D6
Leigh **537**	8 A4
Leweston **28**	*
Lillington **82**	8 A4
Littlebredy **104**	11 E4
Litton Cheney **348**	10 D4
Loders **475**	10 D4
Long Bredy **218**	11 E4
Longburton **433**	8 B4
Long Crichel **97**	9 F4
Longham	13 E3
Lydlinch **410**	8 C4
Lyme Regis **3,566**	10 B4
Lyon's Gate	11 F2

Place	Population	Map ref
Lytchett Matravers	2,871	12 C3
Lytchett Minster & Upton	7,327	12 D4
Maiden Newton	937	11 E3
Mannington		13 E2
Manston	160	8 D3
Mapperton	20	10 D3
Mappowder	190	11 G2
Margaret Marsh	53	8 D3
Marnhull	1,844	8 C3
Marshwood	276	10 B3
Martinstown		11 F4
Melbury Abbas	299	*
Melbury Bubb	66	11 E2
Melbury Osmond	168	11 E2
Melbury Sampford	48	11 E2
Melcombe Bingham		12 A2
Melcombe Horsey	132	*
Melcombe Regis	4,413	11 F6
Melplash		10 D3
Middlemarsh		11 F2
Milborne St Andrew	928	12 B3
Milton Abbas	542	12 A3
Milton on Stour		8 D1
Minterne Magna	191	11 F2
Monkton Up Wimborne		9 G4
Moor Crichel	167	12 D1
Moordown	7,473	13 E4
Morcombelake		10 C4
Morden	345	12 C3
Moreton	275	12 A5
Mosterton	526	10 C2
Motcombe	928	8 D2
Mudeford	5,693	13 G4
Netherbury	1,085	10 C3
Nether Cerne	20	11 F3
Nether Compton	309	8 A3
Nettlecombe		10 D3
Newtown		13 E4
Norden		12 D5
North Poorton	22	10 D3
North Wootton	48	8 B4
Oborne	116	8 B3
Okeford Fitzpaine	646	8 D4
Osmington	517	11 G5
Osmington Mills		11 G6
Over Compton	157	*
Owermoigne	434	12 A5
Pamphill	616	*
Parkstone	9,639	13 E4
Parley Cross		13 F3
Pentridge	190	9 G3
Piddlehinton	468	11 G3
Piddletrenthide	646	11 G3
Pilsdon	51	10 C3
Pimperne	933	9 E4
Plush		11 G2
Poole	91,921	12 D4
Portesham	667	11 E5
Portland	12,742	10 B5
Powerstock	371	10 D3
Poxwell	43	12 A5
Poyntington	145	8 B3
Preston		11 G5
Puddletown	1,130	11 H4
Pulham	168	*
Puncknowle	451	11 E5
Purse Caundle	113	8 B3
Rampisham	140	11 E2
Ridge		12 C5
Rodden		11 E5
Ryall		10 C4
Ryme Intrinseca	140	11 E1
St Ives (with St Leonard's)	6,534	13 F2
Salwayash		10 C3
Sandbanks		13 E5
Sandford Orcas	206	8 A3
Seaborough	56	10 C2
Shaftesbury	6,203	8 D2
Shapwick	195	12 C2
Sherborne	7,606	8 A3
Shillingstone	944	8 D4
Shipton Gorge	344	10 D4
Silton	139	*
Sixpenny Handley	1,039	9 F3
Slepe		12 C4
Southbourne	8,310	13 F4
South Perrott	244	10 D2
Southwell		10 B6
Spetisbury	543	12 C2
Stalbridge	2,344	8 C3
Stalbridge Weston		8 B3
Stanbridge		12 D2
Stanton St Gabriel	97	*
Stapehill	1,843	13 E3
Steeple	94	12 C6
Stinsford	324	11 G4
Stoborough		12 C5
Stoborough Green		12 C5
Stockwood	27	*
Stoke Abbott	215	10 C3
Stokeford		12 B5
Stoke Wake	54	*
Stourpaine	598	*
Stour Provost	529	8 D3
Stour Row		8 D3
Stourton Caundle	377	8 B3
Stratton	316	11 F4
Stubhampton		9 E4
Studland	471	13 E5
Sturminster Common		8 D4
Sturminster Marshall	1,492	12 D3
Sturminster Newton	2,579	8 C4
Sutton Waldron	190	9 E3
Swanage	9,037	13 E6
Swyre	110	10 D5
Sydling St Nicholas	392	11 F3
Symondsbury	1,092	10 C4
Tadden		12 D2
Tarrant Crawford	24	12 C2
Tarrant Gunville	248	9 F4
Tarrant Hinton	185	9 F4
Tarrant Keyneston	290	12 C2
Tarrant Launceston	608	9 F4
Tarrant Monkton	1,293	12 C1
Tarrant Rawston	55	12 C2
Tarrant Rushton	108	12 C2
Three Legged Cross		13 F2
Thorncombe (Beaminster)	624	10 B2
Thorncombe (Blandford F.)		12 B2
Thornford	804	8 A4
Tincleton	139	12 A4
Todber	86	8 D3
Toller Fratrum	27	11 E3
Toller Porcorum	345	11 E3
Tolpuddle	317	12 A4
Trent	304	8 A3
Trickett's Cross	5,338	13 F3
Turners Puddle	57	12 B4
Turnworth	65	12 B2
Tyneham		12 C6
Up Cerne	11	11 F2
Up Sydling		11 F2
Upwey		11 F5
Verwood	10,446	9 H4
Walditch		10 D4
Wareham	5,644	12 C5
Wareham St Martin	2,544	*
Warmwell	98	12 A5
Waterloo		13 E4
West Bay		10 C4
West Bexington		10 D5
Westbourne	6,832	13 E4
West Chelborough	33	10 D2
West Compton	37	11 E4
West Holme		12 C5
West Knighton	408	11 G5
West Lulworth	838	12 B6
West Milton		10 D3
West Moors	6,878	13 E2
Weston		10 B6
West Orchard	77	8 D3
West Parley	3,510	13 F3
West Stafford	244	11 G4
West Stour	159	8 C2
Weymouth	44,098	11 F6
Whatcombe		12 B3
Whitcombe	64	*
Whitchurch Canonicorum	669	10 B3
White Lackington		11 G3
Wick		13 F4
Wimborne Minster	6,292	12 D3
Wimborne St Giles	368	9 G4
Winfrith Newburgh	705	12 B5
Winterborne Carne	47	*
Winterborne Clenston	45	12 B2
Winterborne Herrinsgton	26	11 G5
Winterborne Houghton	198	12 B2
Winterborne Kingston	491	12 B3
Winterborne Monkton	63	11 F5
Winterborne St Martin	769	*
Winterborne Stickland	542	12 B2
Winterborne Whitechurch	594	12 B3
Winterborne Zelston	133	12 C3
Winterbourne Abbas	295	11 F4
Winterbourne Steepleton	282	11 F4
Winton	7,795	13 F4
Witchampton	399	12 D2
Woodlands	537	13 E1
Woodsford	89	12 A4
Woodyates		9 G3
Wool	4,435	12 B5
Woolland	79	12 A2
Wootton Fitzpaine	295	10 B3
Worth Matravers	603	12 D6
Wraxall	41	*
Wyke	2,045	8 D2
Wyke Regis	5,168	10 B5
Wynford Eagle	57	11 E3
Yetminster	1,017	8 A4

Population figures are based upon the 1991 census and relate to the local authority area or parish as constituted at that date Boundaries of the districts are shown on pages 4-5. Places with no population figure form part of a larger local authority area or parish.

Population figures in bold type.

*Place not included on map pages 8-13 due to limitation of space

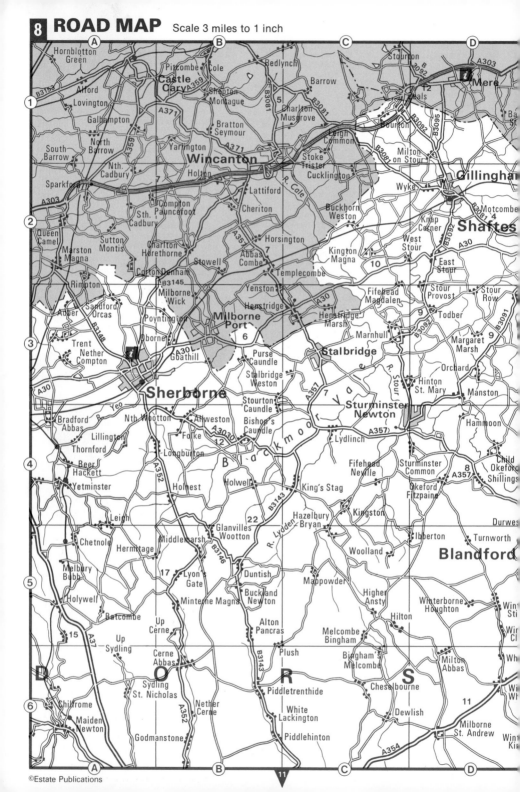

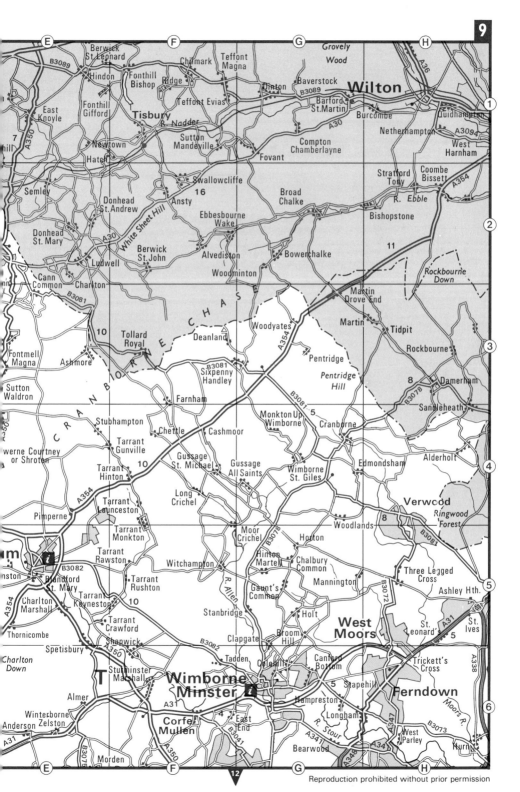

E F G H

B3089 Berwick St.Leonard Chilmark Teffont Magna Grovely Wood

Hindon Fonthill Bishop Ridge Dinton Baverstock **Wilton** A36

East Knoyle Fonthill Gifford Teffont Evias B3089 Barford St.Martin Burcombe Quidhampton 1

A350 **Tisbury** R. Nadder A30 Netherhampton A3094 West Harnham

7 Newtown Sutton Mandeville Compton Chamberlayne Stratford Tony Coombe Bissett A354

hill Hatch Fovant

Semley Swallowcliffe 16 Broad Chalke R. Ebble Bishopstone 2

Donhead St.Andrew Ansty Ebbesbourne Wake 11

White Sheet Hill

Donhead St. Mary A30 Berwick St. John Alvediston Bowerchalke Rockbourne Down

Ludwell Woodminton

Cann Common Charlton Martin Drove End 3

B3081 C Martin Tidpit

10 Tollard Royal Deanland Woodyates Martin Rockbourne

Fontmell Magna Ashmore R Pentridge 8 Damerham

Sutton Waldron A B3081 Sixpenny Handley Pentridge Hill B3078 Sandleheath

Farnham B3081 5 N Alderholt

werne Courtney or Shroten Stubhampton Chettle Cashmoor Monkton Up Wimborne Cranborne B Edmondsham

Tarrant Gunville Gussage St. Michael Gussage All Saints Wimborne St. Giles 4

Tarrant Hinton 10 O Woodlands 8 Verwood

Long Crichel Ringwood Forest

Tarrant Launceston Moor Crichel Horton B3081

Pimperne A354 Tarrant Monkton E Witchampton Chalbury Common Mannington Three Legged Cross

Tarrant Rawston Hinton Martell B3072 Ashley Hth. 5

m i B3082 Gaunt's Common St. Leonard's St. Ives

nston Blandford St. Mary Tarrant Keyneston 10 Stanbridge Holt **West Moors** 5 A31

A354 Charlton Marshall Tarrant Crawford Clapgate Broom Hill Trickett's Cross A338

Thornicombe Shapwick Tadden Colehill Canford Bottom Moors R. 6

Charlton Down Spetisbury A350 B3082 Stapehill **Ferndown**

T Sturminster Marshall **Wimborne Minster** 5 Hampreston Longham

Almer A31 Corfe Mullen East End R. Stour West Parley B3073

Winterborne Zelston Anderson B3041 Bearwood A341 Hurn

A31 Morden B3075 A350

E F G H

12

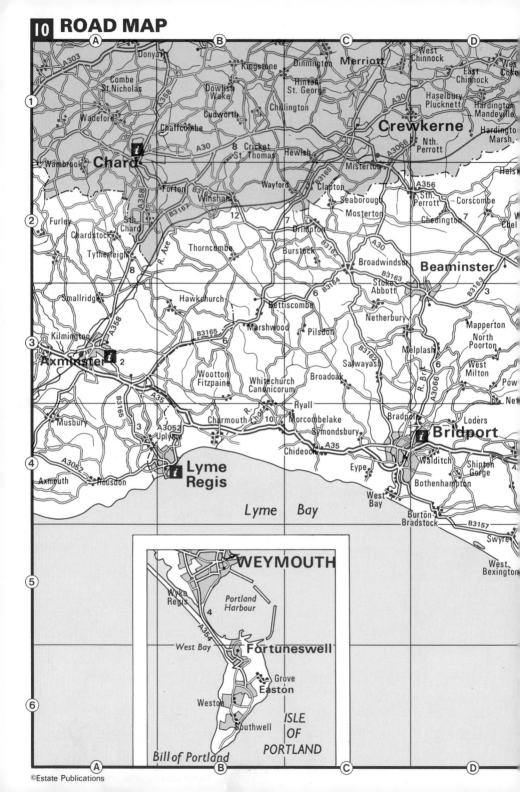

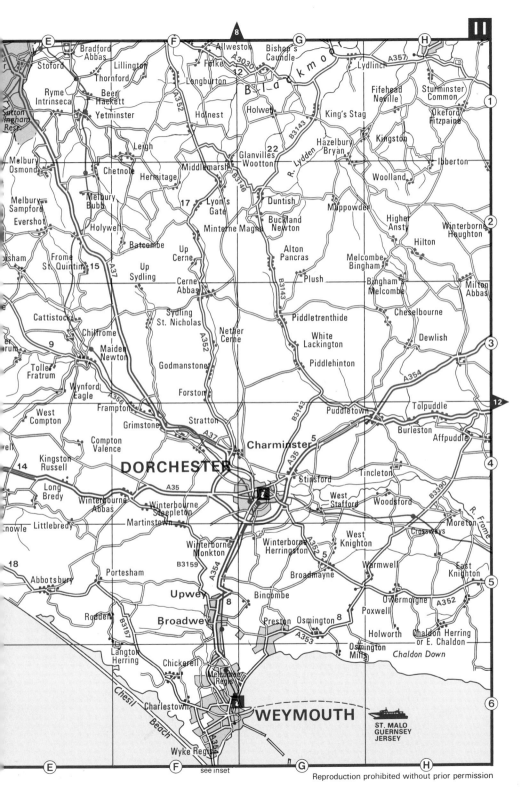

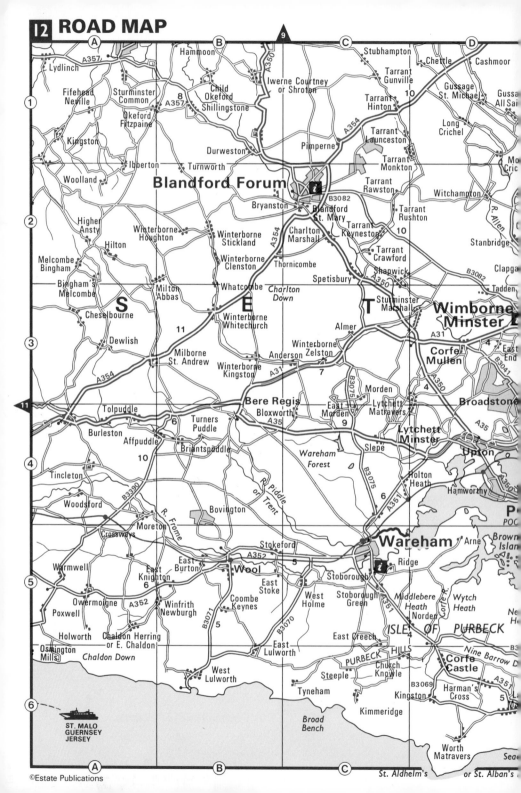

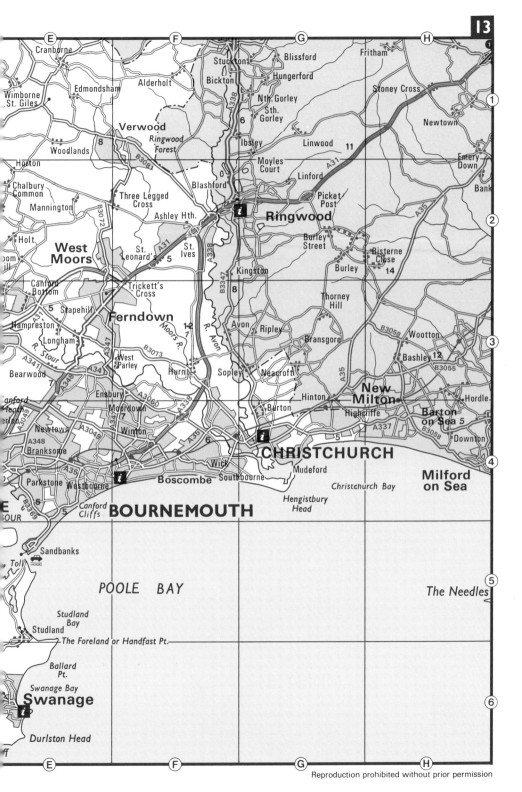

POOLE BAY

BOURNEMOUTH

CHRISTCHURCH

Ringwood

New Milton

Swanage

The Needles

Milford on Sea

Christchurch Bay

Hengistbury Head

Cranborne
Edmondsham
Alderholt
Stuckton
Blissford
Fritham
Wimborne St. Giles
Bickton
Hungerford
Stoney Cross
Nth. Gorley
Verwood
Sth. Gorley
Newtown
Woodlands
Ringwood Forest
Ibsley
Linwood
Emery Down
Horton
Moyles Court
Bank
Chalbury Common
Three Legged Cross
Blashford
Linford
Mannington
Ashley Hth.
Picket Post
Holt
West Moors
St. Leonard's
St. Ives
Kingston
Burley Street
Bisterne Close
Canford Bottom
Trickett's Cross
Burley
Stapehill
Ferndown
Thorney Hill
Hampreston
Longham
Avon
Ripley
Bransgore
Wootton
West Parley
Bearwood
Hurn
Sopley
Neacroft
Bashley
Ensbury
Moordown
Hinton
Burton
Hordle
Newtown
Winton
Highcliffe
Barton on Sea
Branksome
Wick
Mudeford
Downton
Parkstone
Westbourne
Boscombe
Southbourne
Canford Cliffs
Sandbanks
Toll
Studland Bay
Studland
The Foreland or Handfast Pt.
Ballard Pt.
Swanage Bay
Durlston Head

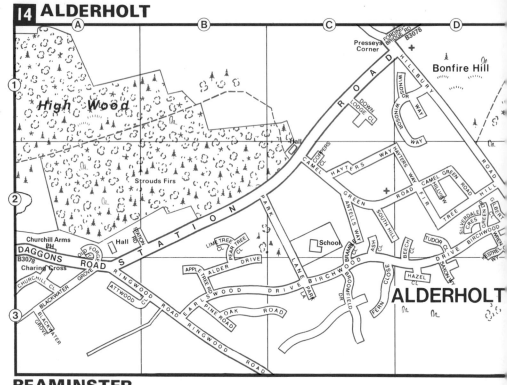

BEAMINSTER

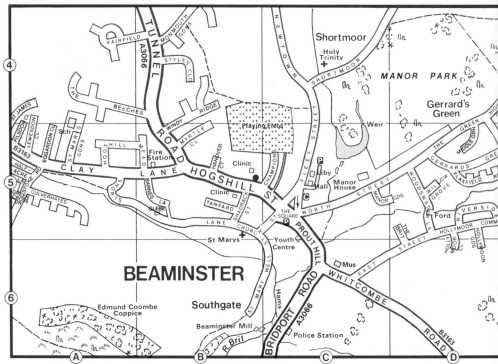

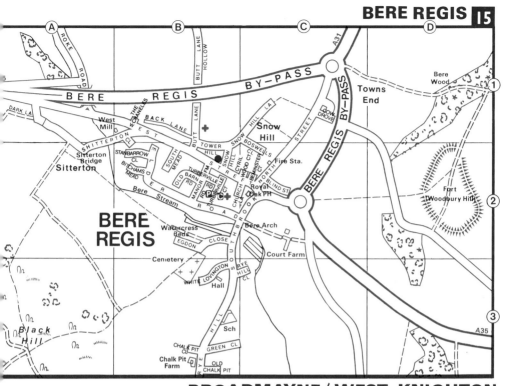

BROADMAYNE / WEST KNIGHTON

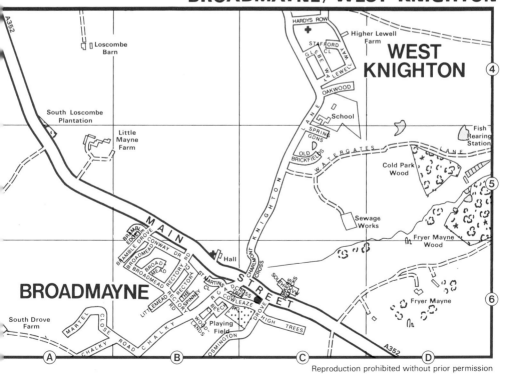

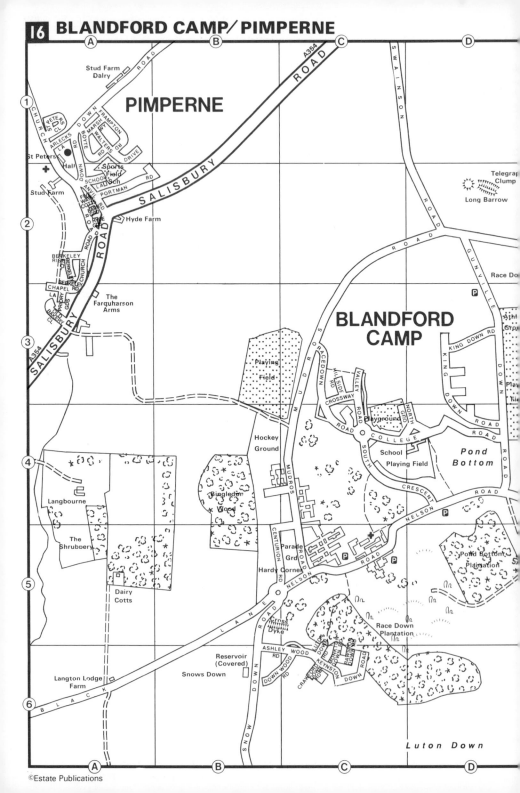

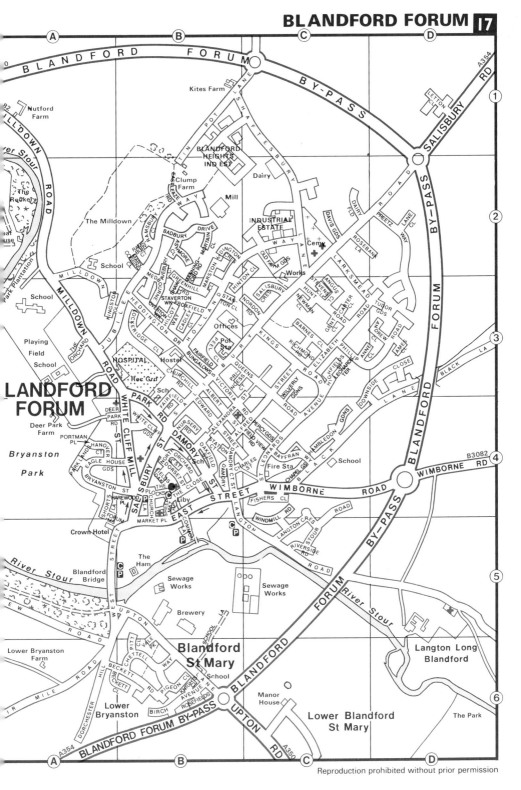

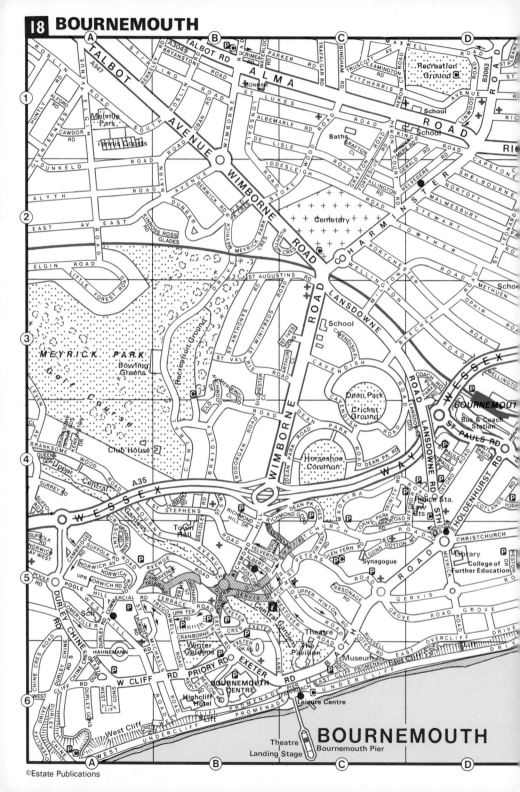

18 BOURNEMOUTH

BOURNEMOUTH

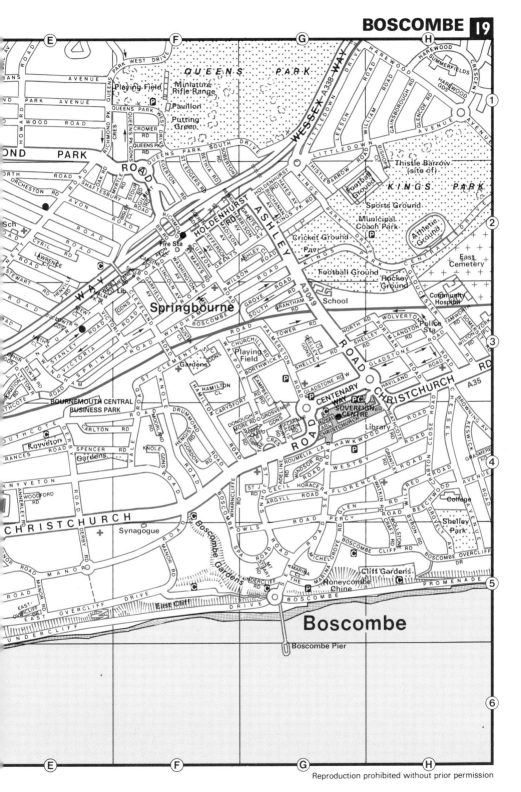

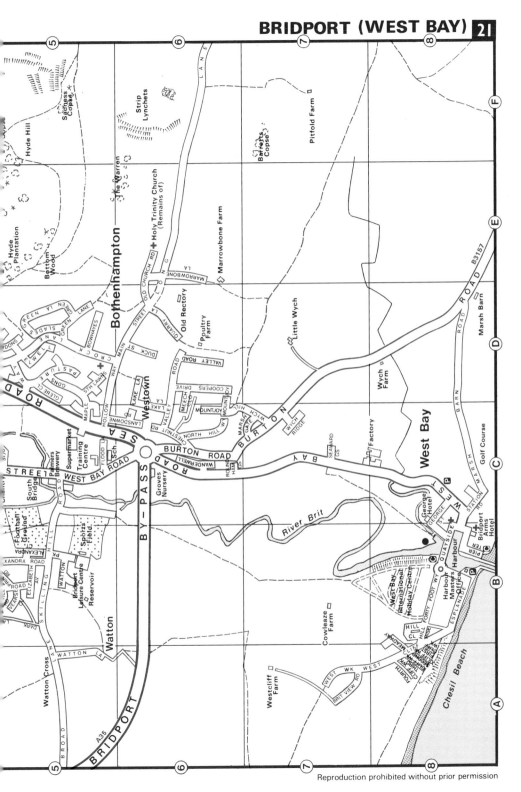

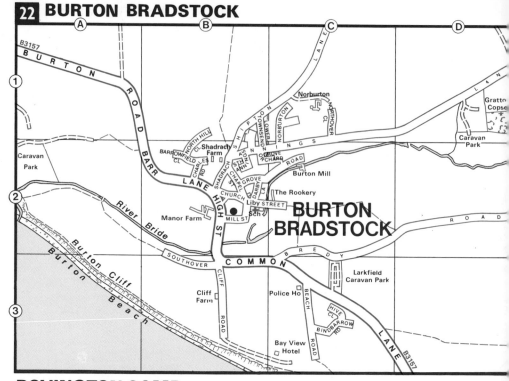

BURTON BRADSTOCK

BOVINGTON CAMP

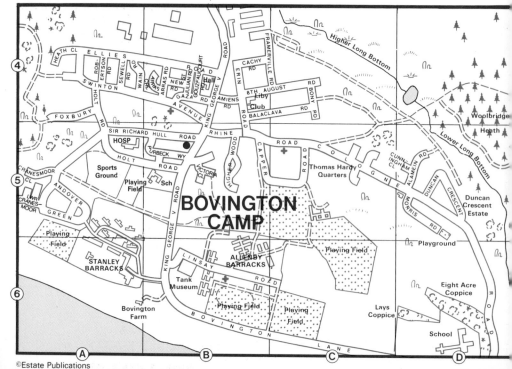

BOVINGTON CAMP

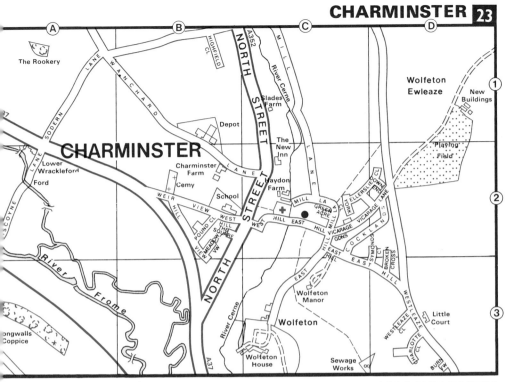

CHARMINSTER

The Rookery
Wolfeton Ewleaze
New Buildings
Slades Farm
The New Inn
Playing Field
Lower Wrackleford
Ford
Charminster Farm
Cemy
Depot
School
Haydon Farm
Green Acre
Little Court
River Frome
Wolfeton Manor
Wolfeton
Longwalls Coppice
River Cerne
Wolfeton House
Sewage Works

CHARMOUTH

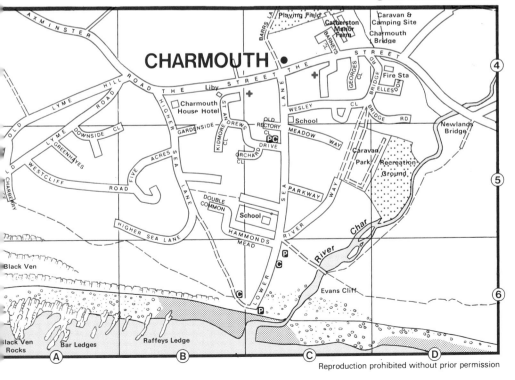

CHARMOUTH

Playing Field
Carberston Manor Farm
Caravan & Camping Site
Charmouth Bridge
Fire Sta
Charmouth House Hotel
Old Rectory
School
Wesley
Newlands Bridge
Caravan Park
Recreation Ground
Double Common
School
Hammonds Mead
River Char
Black Ven
Evans Cliff
Black Ven Rocks
Bar Ledges
Raffeys Ledge

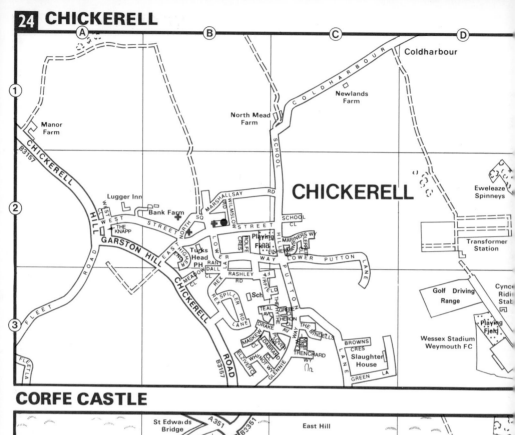

CORFE CASTLE

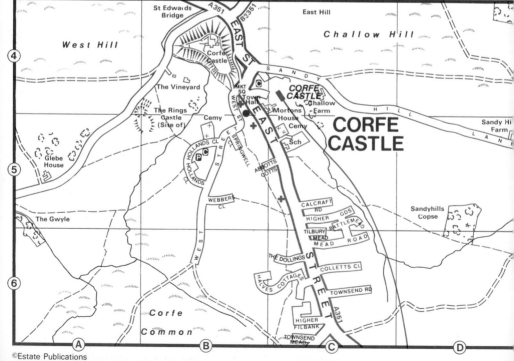

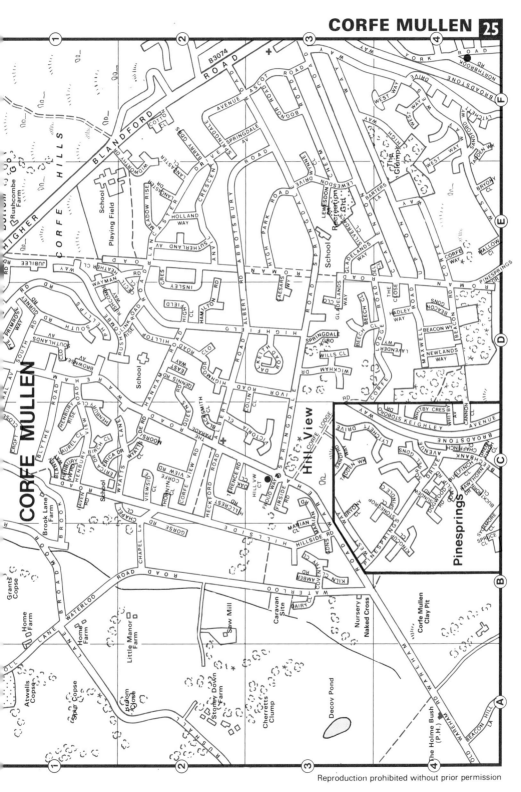

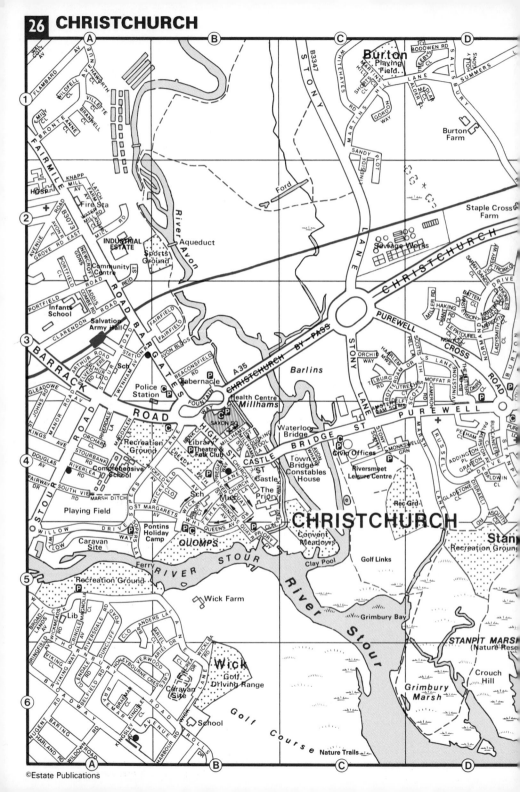

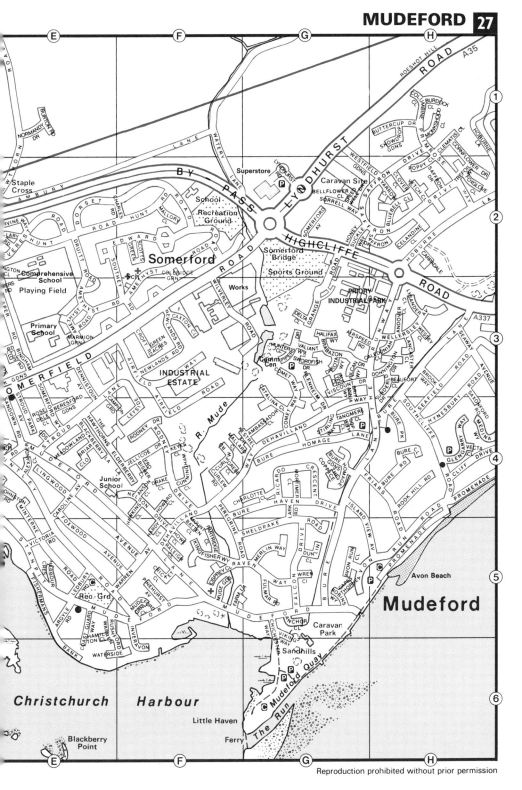

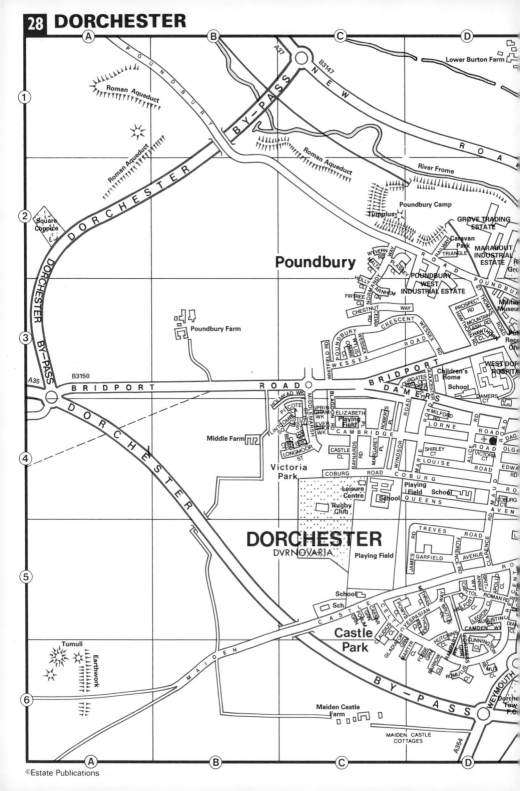

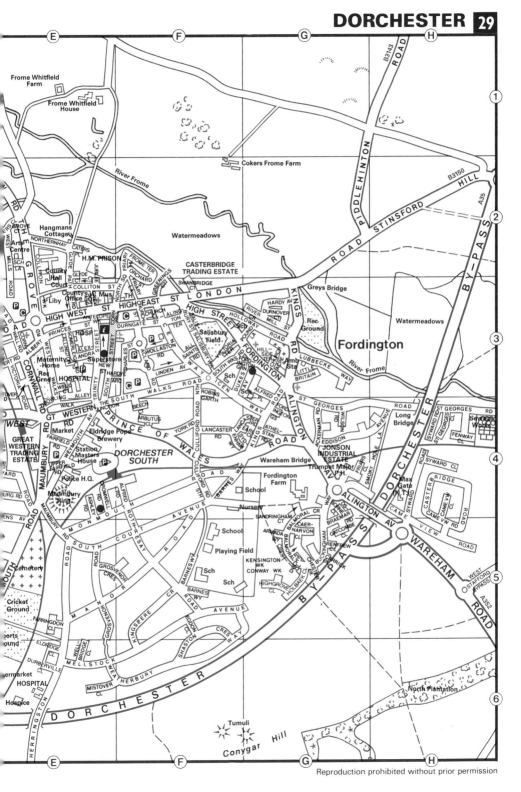

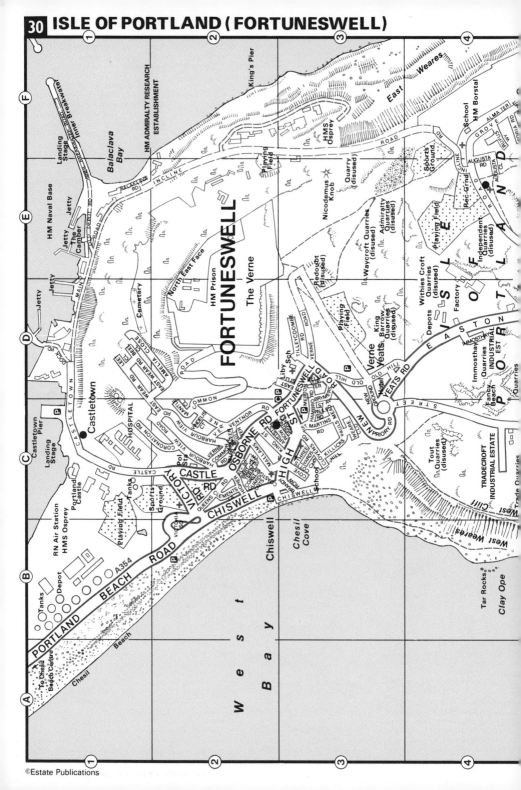

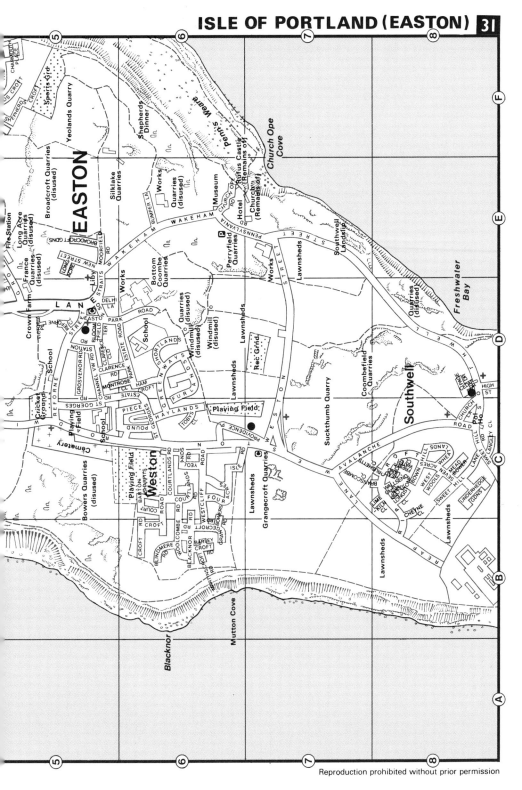

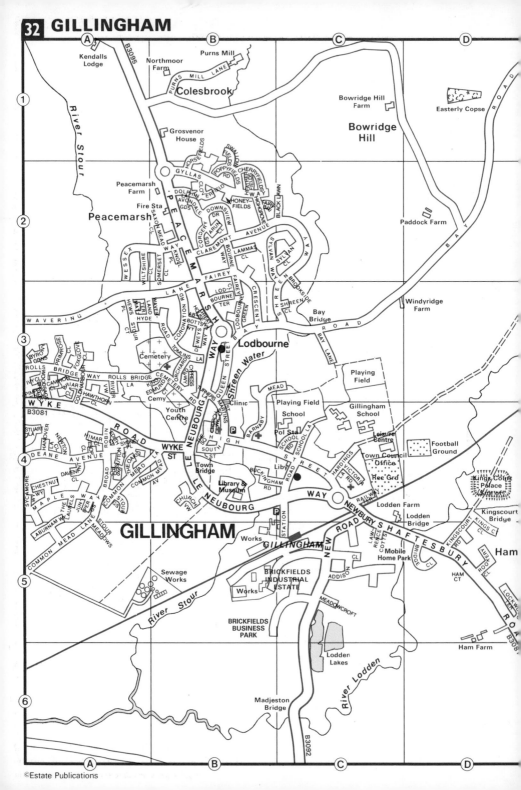

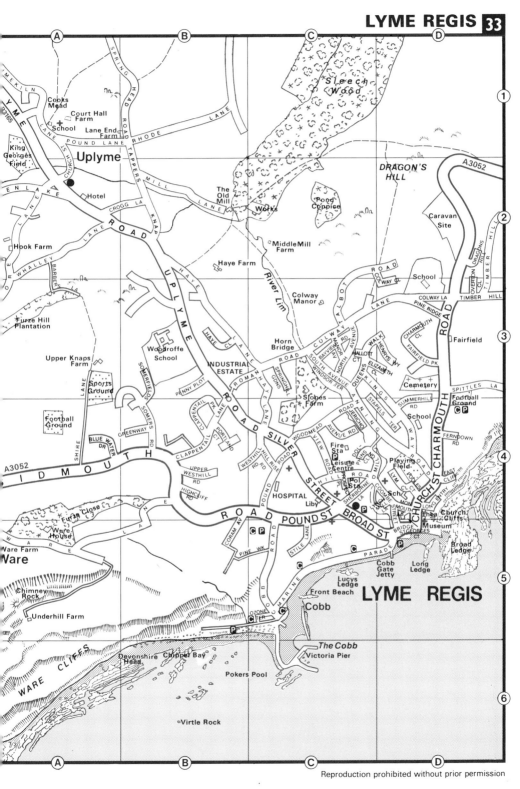

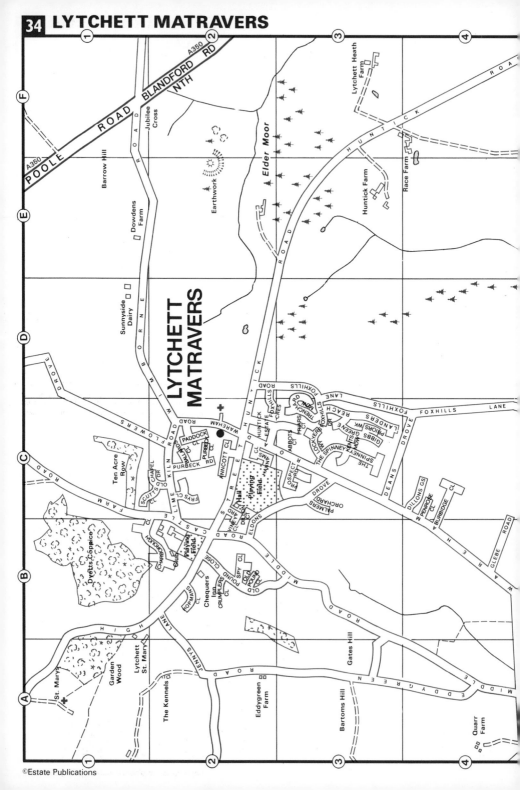

LYTCHETT MATRAVERS

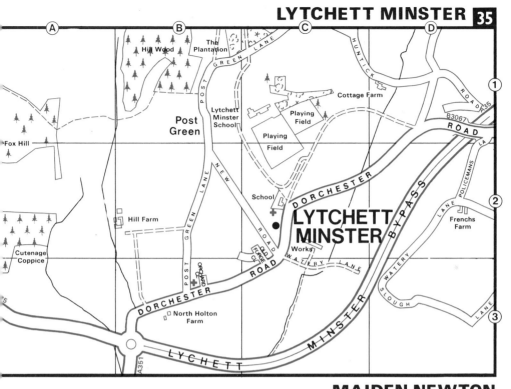

MAIDEN NEWTON

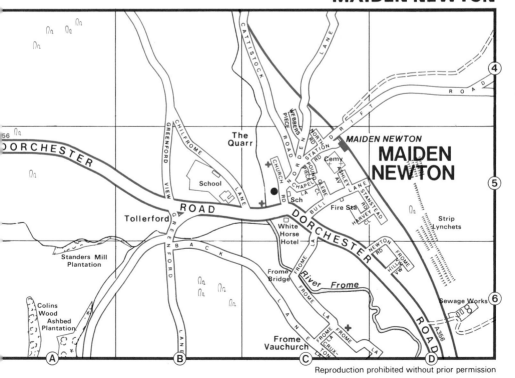

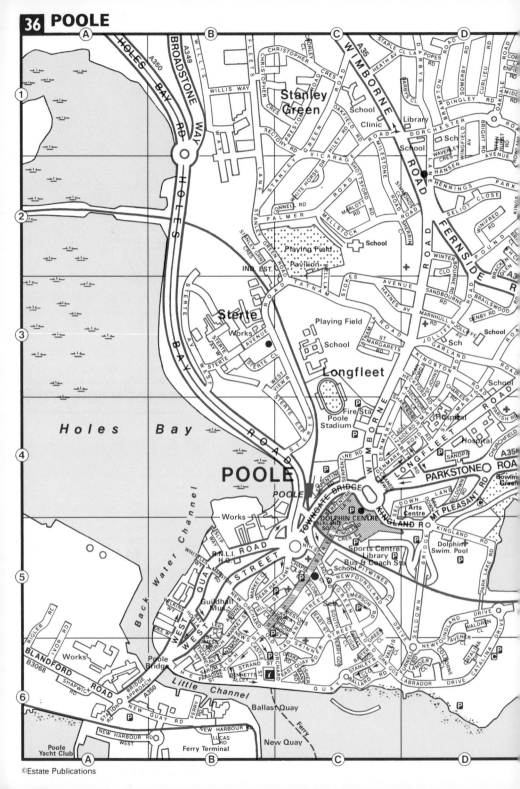

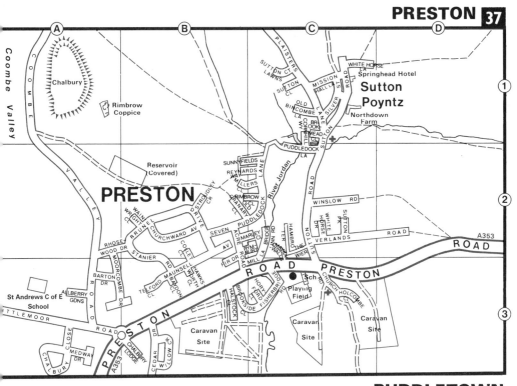

PRESTON

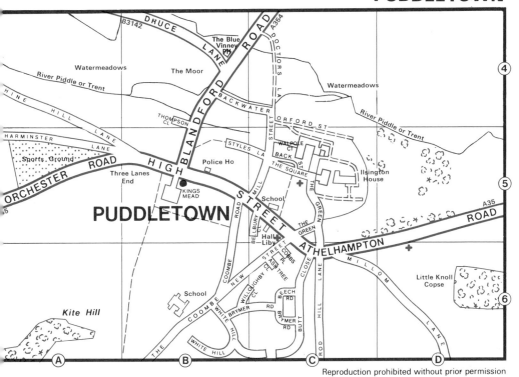

PUDDLETOWN

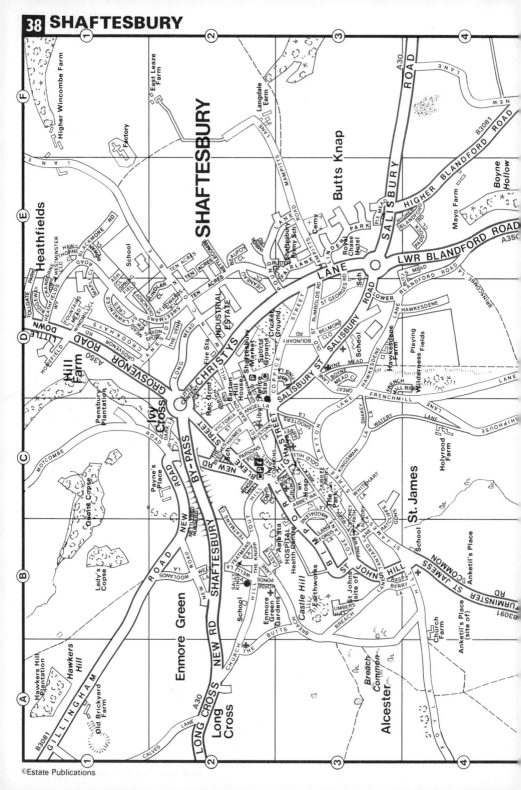

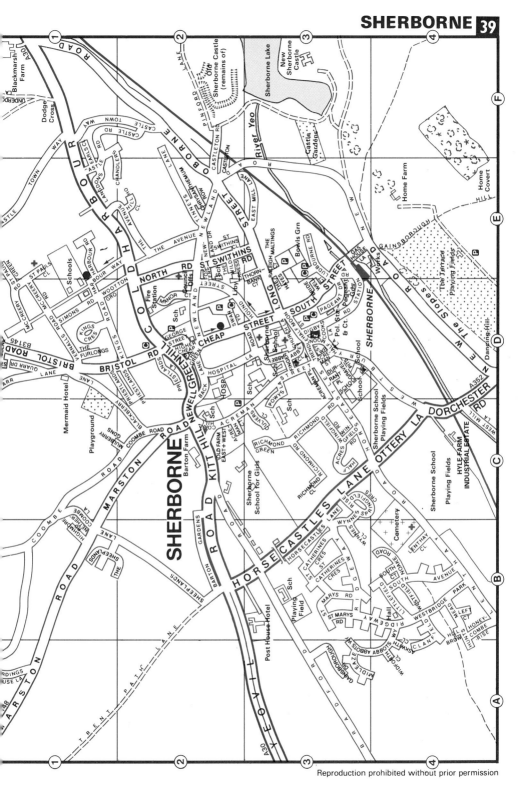

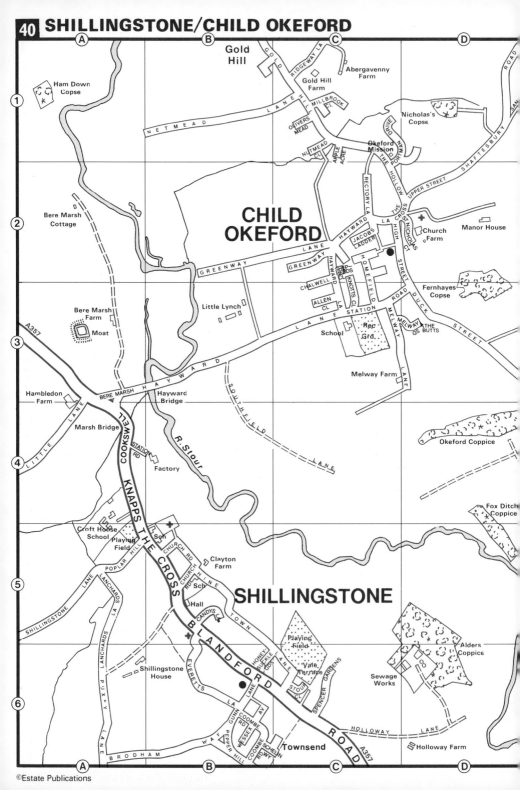

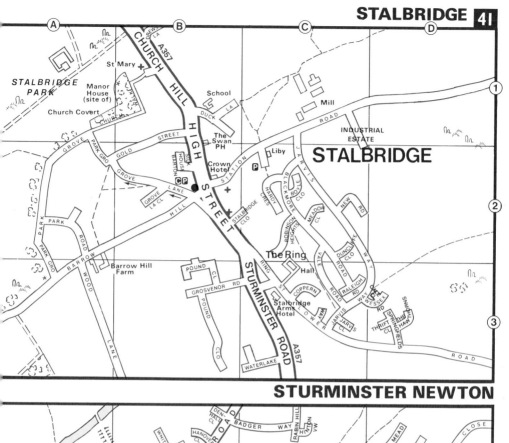

STALBRIDGE

STURMINSTER NEWTON

STURMINSTER NEWTON

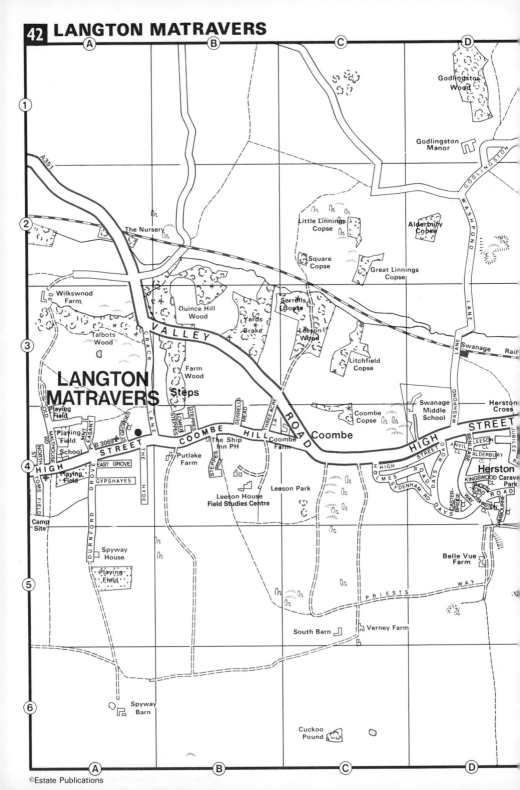

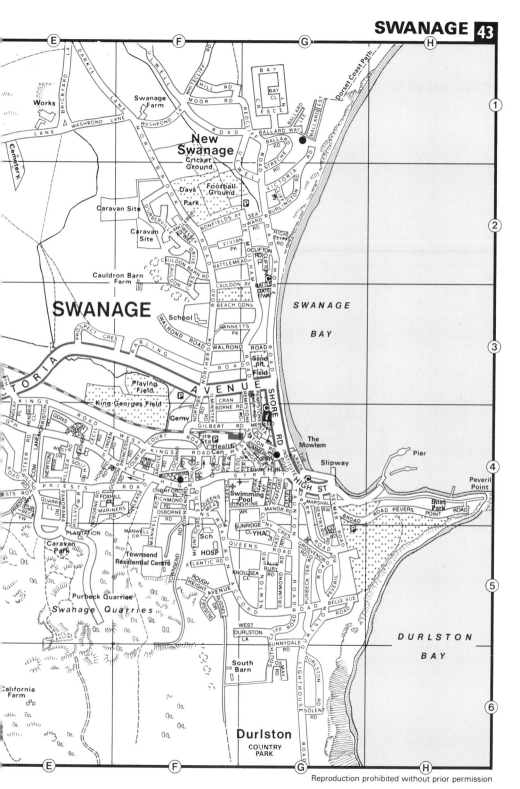

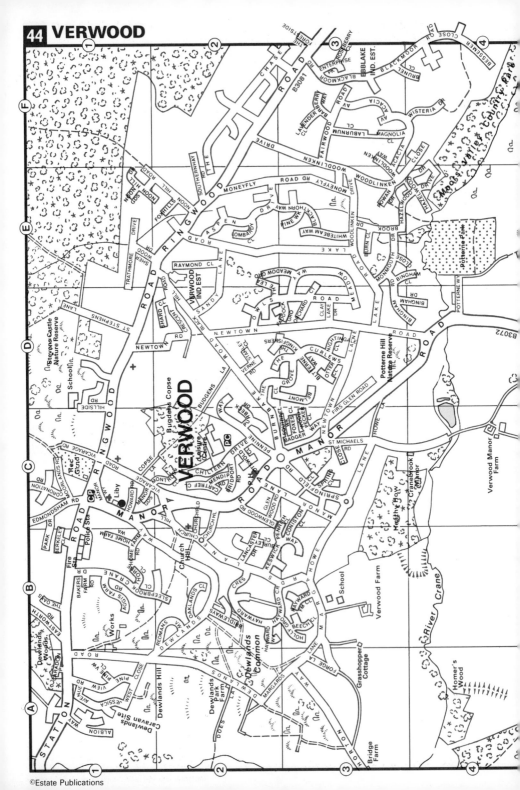

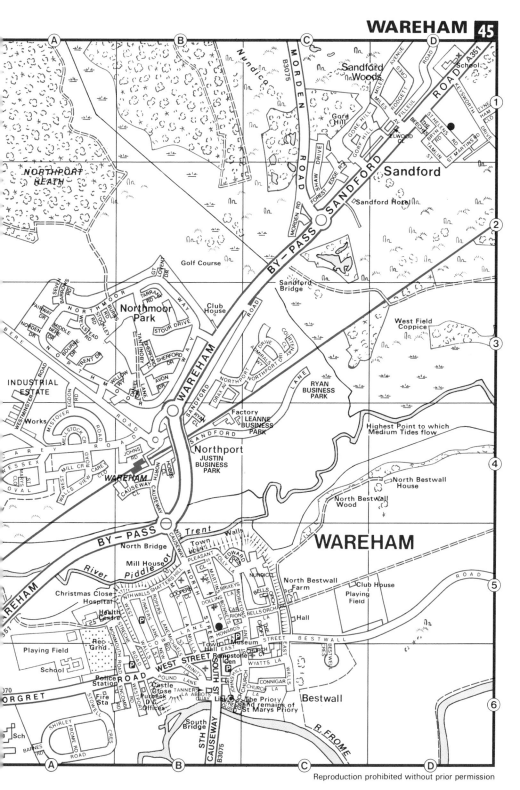

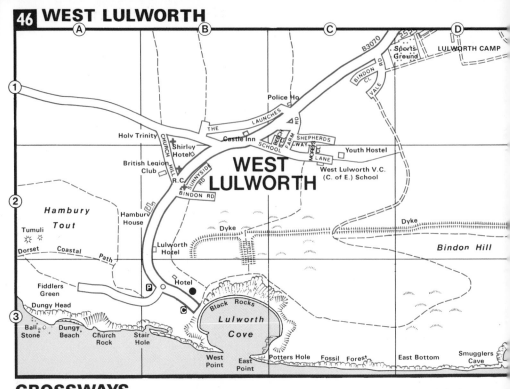

WEST LULWORTH

Holy Trinity
Shirley Hotel
British Legion Club
R.C.
CHURCH HILL
SUNNYSIDE RD
BINDON RD
Castle Inn
Police Ho
THE LAUNCHES
SCHOOL LANE
FARM RD
SHEPHERDS
FALWAY
WEST
Youth Hostel
West Lulworth V.C. (C. of E.) School
B3070
Sports Ground
LULWORTH CAMP
BINDON CL
BINDON VALE RD

Hambury Tout
Hambury House
Tumuli
Dorset Coastal Path
Dyke
Dyke
Bindon Hill

Lulworth Hotel
Fiddlers Green
Dungy Head
Ball Stone
Dungy Beach
Church Rock
Stair Hole
Hotel
P
C

Black Rocks
Lulworth Cove
West Point
East Point
Potters Hole
Fossil Forest
East Bottom
Smugglers Cave

CROSSWAYS

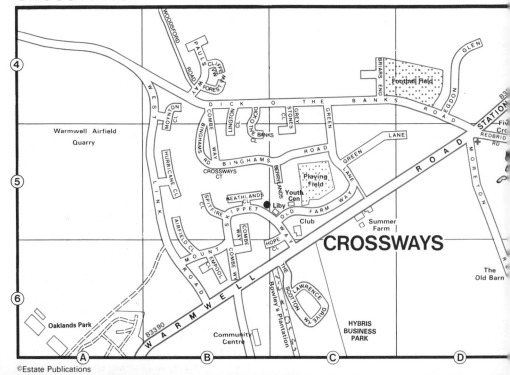

Warmwell Airfield
Quarry

WOODSFORD ROAD
PAULS CLIFF
FOREST W.
ROAD
WEST
LINK
UNION CL.
COMBE WAY
BINGHAMS RD
LINGTON CL.
DICK O THE
BANKS
GREY STONES CL.
DICK O THE BANKS
THE BANKS
GREEN ROAD
LANE
BINGHAMS
CROSSWAYS CT
BERRYANDS
GREEN LANE
GREEN LANE
OLD FARM WAY
Football Field
HOGDON ROAD
GLEN
STATION
Five Cro
REDBRID
RD
MORETON
B3

Playing Field
Youth Cen
Liby
Club
Summer Farm
ROAD
CROSSWAYS
The Old Barn

HURRICANE CL.
AIRFIELD ROAD
SPITFIRE CL.
HEATHLANDS CL.
SKIPPET
COMBE WAY
MOUNT
AIRFIELD COURT
EMPOOL
COMBE WAY
HOPE CL.
THE
WARMWELL
ROAD
B3390
Oaklands Park
Community Centre
BOWLEY'S Plantation
SCOTTON DRIVE
LAWRENCE DRIVE W.
HYBRIS BUSINESS PARK

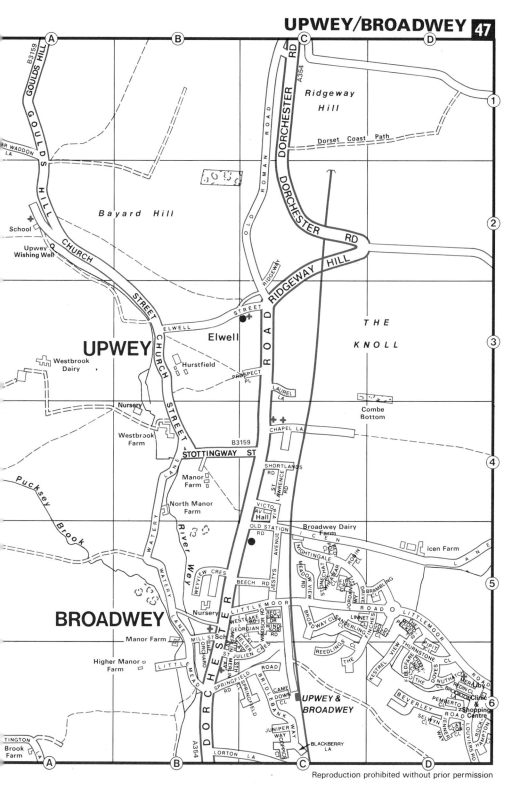

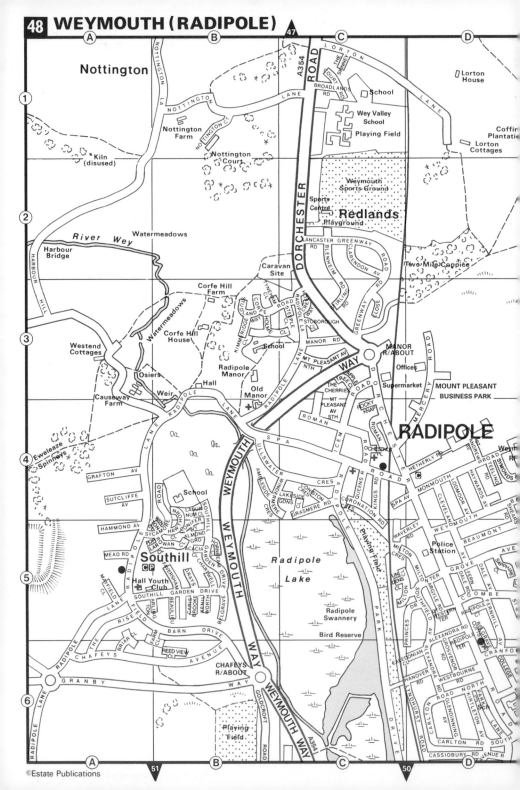

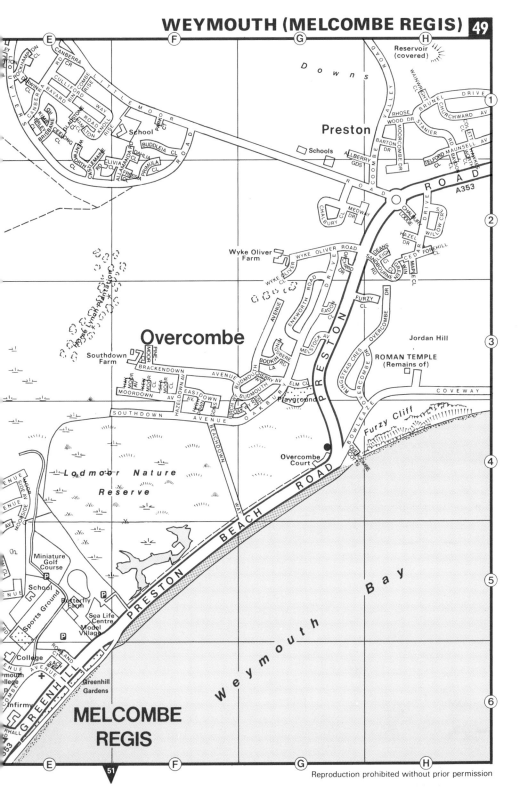

Reservoir
(covered)

Preston

Schools

Downs

Preston

Wyke Oliver
Farm

Overcombe

Horse Lynch Plantation

Southdown
Farm

ROMAN TEMPLE
(Remains of)

Jordan Hill

COVEWAY

Furzy Cliff

Overcombe
Court

Lodmoor Nature

Reserve

Miniature
Golf
Course

School

Sports Ground

Butterfly
Farm

Sea Life
Centre
Model
Village

College

mouth
llege

Infirmary

Greenhill
Gardens

MELCOMBE
REGIS

Weymouth Bay

PRESTON BEACH ROAD

GREENHILL

48

©Estate Publications

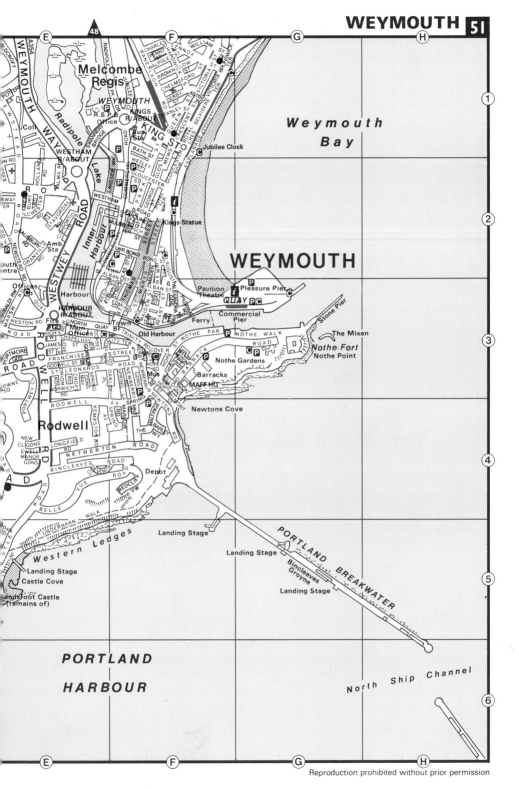

Weymouth Bay

WEYMOUTH

Melcombe Regis

Jubilee Clock

Kings Statue

Pavilion Theatre
Pleasure Pier
QUAY
Commercial Pier
Ferry
Old Harbour
The Mixen
Stone Pier
Nothe Fort
Nothe Point
Nothe Walk
Nothe Gardens
Barracks
MAFF HQ
Mus
Newtons Cove

Rodwell

Depot

Landing Stage
Landing Stage
Bincleaves Groyne
Landing Stage
PORTLAND BREAKWATER

Western Ledges
Landing Stage
Castle Cove
ndsfoot Castle
(remains of)

PORTLAND

HARBOUR

North Ship Channel

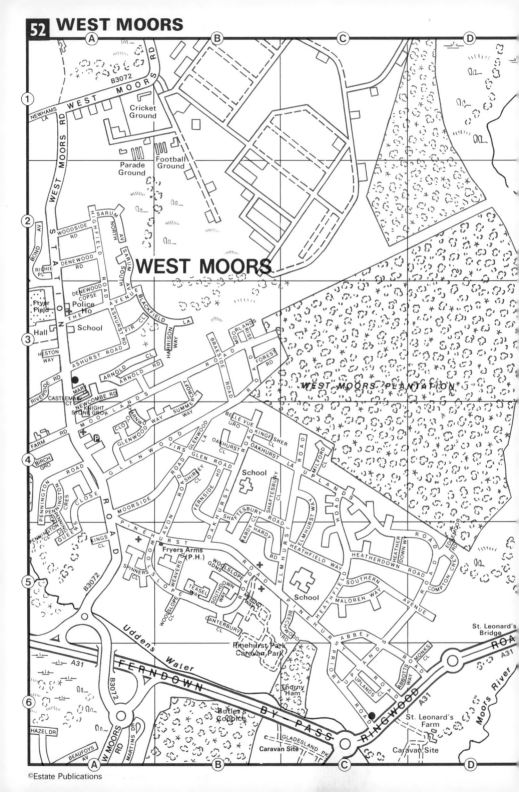

WEST MOORS

WEST MOORS PLANTATION

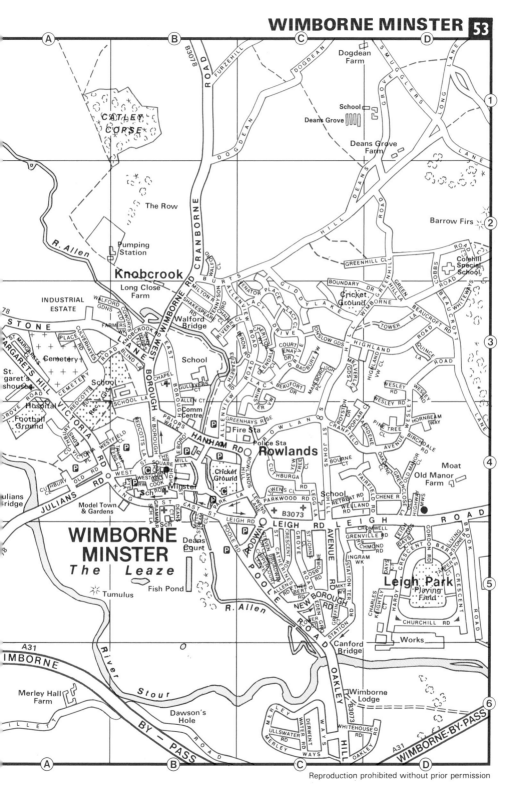

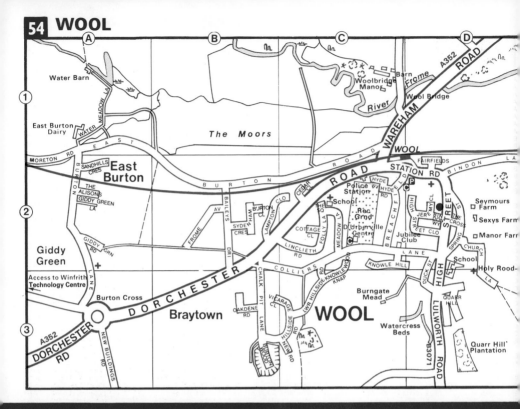

A - Z INDEX TO STREETS
With Postcodes

BLANDFORD FORUM

Albert St. DT11 17 B3
Alexandra St. DT11 17 B4
Alfred St. DT11 17 B4
Andrew Clo. DT11 17 D3
Angus Clo. DT11 17 C3
Anne Clo. DT11 17 C3
Ashmore Clo. DT11 17 B2
Avebury Ct. DT11 17 B2
Badbury Dri. DT11 17 B2
Barnes Clo. DT11 17 C3
Bayfran Way. DT11 17 C4
Beckett Clo. DT11 17 A6
Beckett Rd. DT11 17 A6
Birch Av. DT11 17 B6
Black La. DT11 17 C4
Blandford Forum By-Pass. DT11 17 A1
Bryanston St. DT11 17 A4
Cadley Clo. DT11 17 B3
Carter Clo. DT11 17 C3
Chapel Gdns. DT11 17 C4
Charles St. DT11 17 B4
Chettell Way. DT11 17 B6
Church La. DT11 17 B4
Churchill Rd. DT11 17 B3
Common La. DT11 17 B5
Dairy Field. DT11 17 C2
Damory. DT11 17 B4
Damory Ct St. DT11 17 B4
Damory St. DT11 17 B4
Davis Gdns. DT11 17 C2
Deer Park Rd. DT11 17 A4
Dorchester Hill. DT11 17 A6
Dorset St. DT11 17 B4
Downside Clo. DT11 17 C3
Eagle House Gdns. DT11 17 A4
East St. DT11 17 B4
*East Street La, The Close. DT11 17 B4
Eastleaze Rd. DT11 17 B2
Edward St. DT11 17 B4
Elizabeth Rd. DT11 17 C3
Fair Mile Rd. DT11 17 A6
Fairfield Bungalows. DT11 17 B3
Fairfield Rd. DT11 17 B3
Field View Rd. DT11 17 C4
Fields Oak. DT11 17 B4
Fishers Clo. DT11 17 C4
Forum Mews. DT11 17 A4
Froxfield. DT11 17 B3
Gent Clo. DT11 17 C3
Greenhill Rd. DT11 17 B2
Hambledon Gdns. DT11 17 C4
Hanover Ct. DT11 17 A4
Harewood Pl. DT11 17 B4
Heddington Dri. DT11 17 B3
Highfields. DT11 17 C3
Hilcot Way. DT11 17 B3
Hinton Clo. DT11 17 B3
Holland Way. DT11 17 B3
Hunt Rd. DT11 17 C3
INDUSTRIAL ESTATES:
Blandford Heights Ind Est. DT11 17 B1
James Clo. DT11 17 D3
Jubilee Way. DT11 17 A3
Kings Rd. DT11 17 C3
Kingston Clo. DT11 17 A3
Knights Clo. DT11 17 B6
Lane Clo. DT11 17 D2
Langton Cres. DT11 17 C5
Langton Rd. DT11 17 B4
Larksmead. DT11 17 C2
Letton Clo. DT11 17 D1
Lidington Cres. DT11 17 B3
Lockeridge Clo. DT11 17 B3
Manningford Rd. DT11 17 B2
Market Pl. DT11 17 B5
Marston Clo. DT11 17 B3
Mary Cossins Clo. DT11 17 B2
Medbourne. DT11 17 B2
Milldown. DT11 17 A2
Milldown Rd. DT11 17 A1
Mortain Clo. DT11 17 B2
New Rd. DT11 17 A5
Newman Clo. DT11 17 C3
Nordon Rd. DT11 17 C3
North Pl. DT11 17 B4
Nursery Rd. DT11 17 B4
Oakfield St. DT11 17 B4
Old Farm Gdns. DT11 17 C2
Orchard St. DT11 17 B4
Overton Wk. DT11 17 B3
Park Lands. DT11 17 A4
Park Rd. DT11 17 B3
Peel Clo. DT11 17 B3
Percy Gdns. DT11 17 C4
Phillip Rd. DT11 17 C3
Pigeon Clo. DT11 17 B6
Pitt Clo. DT11 17 B6
Portman Pl. DT11 17 A4
Preetz Way. DT11 17 D2
Princess Ct. DT11 17 B3
Queens Rd. DT11 17 B3
Ramsbury Clo. DT11 17 B2
Ramsbury Ct. DT11 17 B2
Richmond Rd. DT11 17 C3
Riverside Rd. DT11 17 C5
Rosebank La. DT11 17 C2
Rosefields. DT11 17 B6
St Leonards Av. DT11 17 C4
St Leonards Ter. DT11 17 C3
Salisbury Cres. DT11 17 C3
Salisbury Rd. DT11 17 B3
Salisbury St. DT11 17 B4
School La. DT11 17 B5
Shaftesbury La. DT11 17 B1
Shaw Clo. DT11 17 B3
Sheep Market Hill. DT11 17 B4
Shorts La. DT11 17 A4
*Southern Clo, Birch Av. DT11 17 B6
Stanton Clo. DT11 17 B3
Station Ct. DT11 17 B4
Staverton Walk. DT11 17 B3
Stevens Clo. DT11 17 C3
Stour Rd. DT11 17 C5
The Close. DT11 17 B4
The Orchard. DT11 17 A3
The Plocks. DT11 17 B4
*The Tabernacle, Sheep Market Hill. DT11 17 B4
Tin Pot La. DT11 17 B1
Tudor Gdns. DT11 17 D3
Upton La. DT11 17 B5
Upton Rd. DT11 17 B6
Vale Pk. DT11 17 B5
Victoria Rd. DT11 17 B3
*Wessex Ct, Orchard St. DT11 17 B4
West St. DT11 17 A5
White Cliff Gdns. DT11 17 B4
White Cliff Mill St. DT11 17 B4
Wilverly Gdns. DT11 17 C3
Wimborne Rd. DT11 17 C4
Windmill Rd. DT11 17 C4

BOURNEMOUTH BOSCOMBE

Adeline Rd. BH5 19 G4
Albemarle Rd. BH3 18 B1
Albert Rd. BH1 18 B5
Alford Rd. BH3 18 A1
Allington Rd. BH3 18 C2
Alma Rd. BH9 18 B1
Alyth Rd. BH3 18 A2
Annerley Rd. BH1 19 E4
Arcadia Av. BH8 18 D1
Argyll Rd. BH4 19 G4
Arthur Clo. BH2 18 C3
Ascham Rd. BH8 19 E3
Ashley Clo. BH1 19 G2
Ashley Rd. BH1 19 G2
Austin Clo. BH1 19 F3
Avenue La. BH2 18 B5
Avenue Rd. BH2 18 B5
Avon Clo. BH8 19 F2
Avon Rd. BH8 19 E2
Aylesbury Rd. BH1 19 G4
Bath Rd. BH1 18 C6
Beacon Rd. BH2 18 B6
Beechey Rd. BH8 18 D3
Beechwood Av. BH5 19 H4
Beechwood Gdns. BH5 19 H4
Belvedere Rd. BH3 18 D2
Bennett Rd. BH8 19 E2
Berkeley Rd. BH3 18 A1
Berwick Rd. BH3 18 B2
Bethia Clo. BH8 19 F2
Bethia Rd. BH8 19 F1
Bingham Rd. BH9 18 C1
Bishops Clo. BH7 19 H2
Bodorgan Rd. BH2 18 B4
Bonham Rd. BH9 18 B1
Borthwick Rd. BH1 19 G3
Boscombe Cliff Rd. BH5 19 G5
Boscombe Gro Rd. BH1 19 F3
Boscombe Overcliff Dri. BH5 19 H5
Boscombe Prom. BH5 19 G5
Boscombe Spa Rd. BH5 19 F4
Bourne Av. BH2 18 A4
Bradburne Rd. BH2 18 A5
Braidley Rd. BH2 18 B4
Branksome Wood Gdns. BH2 18 A4
Branksome Wood Rd. BH2 18 A4
Browning Av. BH5 19 H4
Bryanstone Rd. BH3 18 B1
Buchanan Av. BH7 19 G2
Byron Rd. BH5 19 H5
Cambridge Rd. BH2 18 A5
Campbell Rd. BH1 19 G3
Capstone Pl. BH8 19 F2
Capstone Rd. BH8 18 D2
Carlton Rd. BH1 19 E4
Carnarvon Rd. BH1 19 G4
Carysfort Rd. BH1 19 F4
Cavendish Pl. BH1 18 C3
Cavendish Rd. BH1 18 C3
Cawdor Rd. BH3 18 A1
Cecil Av. BH8 19 E1
Cecil Rd. BH5 19 G4
Centenary Way. BH1 19 G3
Central Dri. BH2 18 B4
Charminster Rd. BH8 18 C2
Chatsworth Rd. BH8 18 D2
Chessel Av. BH5 19 H4
Chine Cres. BH2 18 A6
Chine Cres Rd. BH2 18 A6
Christchurch Rd. BH1 18 C5
Churchill Rd. BH1 19 G3
Cleveland Gdns. BH1 19 F3
Cleveland Rd. BH1 19 F3
Coach House Pl. BH1 18 D3
Commercial Rd. BH1 18 A5
Corporation Rd. BH1 19 E3
Cotlands Rd. BH1 18 D4
Crabton Close Rd. BH5 19 H4
Cranborne Rd. BH2 18 B5
Crescent Rd. BH2 18 A5
Crimea Rd. BH9 18 B1
Cromer Rd. BH8 19 F1
Cumnor Rd. BH1 18 C5
Curzon Rd. BH1 19 F2
Cyril Rd. BH8 19 E2
Dalkeith La. BH1 18 B5
De Lisle Rd. BH3 18 B1
Dean Park Cres. BH1 18 C4
Dean Park Rd. BH1 18 C4
Derby Rd. BH1 19 E4
Donoughmore Rd. BH1 19 G4
Drummond Rd. BH1 19 F4
Dunbar Rd. BH3 18 B2
Dunkeld Rd. BH3 18 A2
Durley Chine. BH2 18 A6
Durley Chine Rd. BH2 18 A5
Durley Chine Rd Sth. BH2 18 A6
Durley Gdns. BH2 18 A6
Durley Rd. BH2 18 A5
Durley Rd Sth. BH2 18 A6
Durrant Rd. BH2 18 B4
East Av. BH3 18 A2
East Cliff Prom. BH1 18 C6
East Overcliff Dri. BH1 18 D5
Egerton Gdns. BH8 19 F2
Egerton Rd. BH8 19 F2
Elgin Rd. BH4 18 A1
Elwyn Rd. BH1 19 E3
Exeter Cres. BH2 18 B5
Exeter La. BH2 18 B5
Exeter Park Rd. BH2 18 B5
Exeter Rd. BH 18 B5
Fir Vale Rd. BH1 18 C5
Fitzharris Av. BH9 18 C1
Florence Rd. BH5 19 G4
Fortescue Rd. BH3 18 C2
Frances Rd. BH1 19 E4
Gainsborough Rd. BH7 19 H1
Garfield Av. BH1 19 F3
Gerald Rd. BH3 18 D1
Gervis Pl. BH1 18 B5
Gervis Rd. BH1 18 D5
Gilbert Rd. BH8 19 F2
Gladstone Rd. BH7 19 H3
Gladstone Rd West. BH1 19 G3
Glen Fern Rd. BH1 18 C5
Glen Rd. BH5 19 G4
Glencoe Rd. BH7 19 H1
Glenferness Av. BH4 18 A1
Gloucester Rd. BH7 19 H3
Gordon Rd. BH1 19 F4
Grafton Clo. BH3 18 C1
Grafton Rd. BH3 18 C1
Grantham Rd. BH1 19 G3
Grantley Rd. BH5 19 H4
Grants Av. BH1 19 F2
Grants Clo. BH1 19 G2
Grasmere Rd. BH5 19 H4
Grosvenor Gdns. BH1 19 G4
Grove Rd. BH1 18 C5
Grovely Av. BH5 19 H4
Hahnemann Rd. BH2 18 A6
Hamilton Clo. BH1 19 F3
Hamilton Rd. BH1 19 F3
Harewood Av. BH7 19 H1
Harewood Cres. BH7 19 H1
Harewood Gdns. BH7 19 H1
Harrison Av. BH1 19 F2
Haviland Rd. BH7 19 H3
Hawkwood Rd. BH5 19 G4
Hayes Av. BH7 19 G2
Heathcote Rd. BH5 19 H4
Hengist Rd. BH1 19 F4
Henville Rd. BH8 19 E3
Heron Court Rd. BH3 18 C1
Hinton Rd. BH1 18 C5
Holdenhurst Rd. BH8 19 D4
Horace Rd. BH5 19 G4
Howard Rd. BH8 19 E1
Huntly Rd. BH3 18 A1
Ibsley Clo. BH8 19 F2
Iddesleigh Rd. BH3 18 C2
INDUSTRIAL ESTATES:
Bournemouth Central Business Pk. BH1 19 E4
Jefferson Av. BH1 19 F2
Kensington Dri. BH2 18 A4
Kerley Rd. BH2 18 B6
Keswick Rd. BH5 19 H4
Kings Park Central Dri. BH7 19 G2
Kings Park Dri. BH7 19 G2
Kings Park Rd. BH7 19 G2
Kings Rd. BH3 18 D1
Kinross Rd. BH3 18 A2
Knole Gdns. BH1 19 F4
Knole Rd. BH1 19 F3
Knyveton Rd. BH1 19 E4
Langton Rd. BH7 19 H3
Lansdowne Cres. BH1 18 D5
Lansdowne Gdns. BH1 18 D4
Lansdowne Rd. BH1 18 D4
Lansdowne Rd Sth. BH1 18 D4
Lawrence Ct. BH8 19 E2
Leamington Rd. BH9 18 C1
Leeson Rd. BH7 19 G1
Leven Av. BH4 18 A3
Lincoln Av. BH1 19 F2
Linwood Rd. BH9 18 D1
Little Forest Rd. BH4 18 A3
Littledown Av. BH7 19 G1
Littledown Dri. BH7 19 G1
Lonsdale Rd. BH3 18 B1
Lorne Park Rd. BH1 18 C5
Lowther Gdns. BH8 19 E3
Lowther Rd. BH8 18 D1
Lytton Rd. BH1 19 E3
Madeira Rd. BH1 18 C4
Madison Av. BH1 19 F2
Malmesbury Pk Pl. BH8 19 E3
Malmesbury Pk Rd. BH8 18 D2
Manor Rd. BH1 19 E5
Marina Clo. BH5 19 G5
Maxwell Rd. BH9 18 C1
Melbourne Rd. BH8 19 F3
Merlewood Clo. BH2 18 B3
Methuen Clo. BH8 19 E3
Methuen Rd. BH8 18 D3
Meyrick Park Cres. BH3 18 B2
Meyrick Rd. BH1 18 D5
Michelgrove Rd. BH5 19 G5
Milton Rd. BH8 18 C3
Moorland Rd. BH1 19 F4
Mount Stuart Rd. BH5 19 G5
Myrtle Rd. BH8 19 F2
Nairn Rd. BH3 18 B2
North Rd. BH7 19 G3
Northcote Rd. BH1 19 E3
Nortoft Rd. BH8 18 D2
Norwich Av. BH2 18 A5
Norwich Av W. BH2 18 A5
Norwich Rd. BH2 18 A5
Oak Rd. BH8 19 E2
Oban Rd. BH3 18 B1
Old Christchurch Rd. BH1 18 B5
Ophir Gdns. BH8 19 E3
Ophir Rd. BH8 18 D3
Orchard St. BH2 18 B5
Orcheston Rd. BH8 19 E2
Overcliff Dri. BH6 18 A6
Owls Rd. BH5 19 G5
Oxford Rd. BH8 18 D4
Palmerston Rd. BH1 19 G3
Park Rd. BH8 18 D3
Parker Rd. BH9 18 B1
Parsonage Rd. BH1 18 C5
Percy Rd. BH5 19 G4
Pier Approach. BH1 18 C6
Poole Hill. BH2 18 A5
Poole Rd. BH2 18 A5
Portchester Pl. BH8 18 D3
Portchester Rd. BH8 18 C2
Portman Rd. BH7 19 H3
Post Office Rd. BH1 18 B5
Priory Rd. BH2 18 B6
Purbeck Rd. BH2 18 A5
Queens Gdns. BH2 18 A4
Queens Pk Gdns. BH8 19 F1
Queens Pk Rd. BH8 19 F1
Queens Pk S Dri. BH8 19 F1
Queens Pk W Dri. BH8 19 F1
Randolph Rd. BH1 19 G4
Richmond Bri Rd. BH8 19 F2
Richmond Gdns. BH1 18 C4
Richmond Hill. BH2 18 B5
Richmond Hill Dri. BH2 18 B4
Richmond Pk Av. BH8 18 D1
Richmond Pk Cres. BH8 19 E1
Richmond Pk Rd. BH8 19 D1
Richmond Wood Rd. BH8 18 D1
Roslin Rd. BH3 18 A1
Roslin Rd Sth. BH3 18 A1
Ross Glades. BH3 18 B2
Roumelia La. BH5 19 G4
Royal Arcade. BH1 19 G4
Rushton Cres. BH3 18 C2
Russell Cotes Rd. BH1 18 C5
St Albans Av. BH8 18 D1
St Albans Cres. BH8 18 D1
St Anthonys Rd. BH2 18 B3
St Augustins Rd. BH2 18 B2
St Clements Gdns. BH1 19 F3
St Clements Rd. BH1 19 F3
St Ives Gdns. BH2 18 C3
St Johns Rd. BH5 19 G4
St Ledgers Pl. BH8 19 F2
St Ledgers Rd. BH8 19 F2
St Leonards Rd. BH8 18 D2
St Lukes Rd. BH3 18 B1
St Marys Rd. BH1 19 F2
St Michaels Rd. BH2 18 A5
St Pauls La. BH8 18 D4
St Pauls Pl. BH8 18 D4
St Pauls Rd. BH8 18 D4
St Peters Rd. BH1 18 C5
St Stephens Rd. BH2 18 B4
St Stephens Way. BH2 18 B4
St Swithuns Rd. BH1 18 D4
St Valerie Rd. BH2 18 B3
St Winifreds Rd. BH2 18 B3
Salisbury Rd. BH1 19 G4
Sea Rd. BH5 19 G5
Shaftesbury Rd. BH8 19 E2
Shelbourne Rd. BH8 18 D2
Shelley Clo. BH1 19 G3
Shelley Gdns. BH1 19 G3
Shelley Rd. BH1 19 G3
Silchester Clo. BH2 18 B3
Soberton Rd. BH8 19 F1
Somerset Rd. BH7 19 H3
Somerville Rd. BH2 18 A5
South Rd, Boscombe. BH1 19 G3
South Rd, Bournemouth. BH1 18 C6
Southcote Rd. BH1 19 E4
Spencer Rd. BH1 19 E4
Spring Rd. BH1 19 E3
Stafford Rd. BH1 18 D4
Stanley Rd. BH1 19 E3
Stewart Clo. BH8 19 E3
Stewart Rd. BH8 18 D2
Stirling Rd. BH3 18 A1
Stoke Wood Rd. BH3 18 C2
Stour Rd. BH8 19 F2
Suffolk Rd. BH2 18 A5
Suffolk Rd Sth. BH2 18 A4
Summerfields. BH7 19 H1
Surrey Rd. BH4 18 A4

Fairfield. DT3 24 B3
Fishermans Clo. DT3 24 C2
Fleet La. DT3 24 A3
Fleet Rd. DT3 24 A3
Garston Hill. DT3 24 A2
Glennie Way. DT3 24 C3
Grebe Clo. DT3 24 C3
Green La. DT3 24 C3
Heron Clo. DT3 24 C3
Higher End. DT3 24 B2
Lerrett Clo. DT3 24 C2
Lower Putton La. DT3 24 C2
Lower Way. DT3 24 B2
Mariners Way. DT3 24 C2
Marshallsay Rd. DT3 24 B2
Maskew Clo. DT3 24 B3
Meadow Clo. DT3 24 B3
North Sq. DT3 24 C3
Plover Dri. DT3 24 C3
Putton La. DT3 24 C3
Randall Clo. DT3 24 B3
Rashley Rd. DT3 24 B3
Rex La. DT3 24 B3
Rolfe Cres. DT3 24 C2
School Clo. DT3 24 C2
School Hill. DT3 24 C1
Spiller Rd. DT3 24 B3
Teal Av. DT3 24 B3
The Hythe. DT3 24 C3
Trenchard Way. DT3 24 C3
West Clo. DT3 24 A2
West St. DT3 24 A2
Whynot Way. DT3 24 A2
Wilmslow Rd. DT3 24 B2

CHRISTCHURCH

Addington Pl. BH23 26 D4
Addiscombe Rd. BH23 26 A3
Airfield Rd. BH23 27 F4
Airfield Way. BH23 27 F3
Airspeed Rd. BH23 27 G3
Alder Clo. BH23 26 D1
Alexander Clo. BH23 27 E4
Ambassador Clo. BH23 27 G4
Ambury La. BH23 27 E2
Amethyst Rd. BH23 27 E3
Amsterdam Sq. BH23 26 C4
Anchor Clo. BH23 27 G5
Andover Clo. BH23 27 H3
Anne Clo. BH23 26 A1
Anson Clo. BH23 27 F4
Argyle Rd. BH23 27 E5
Ariel Clo. BH6 26 B5
Ariel Dri. BH6 26 B6
Arthur La. BH23 26 A3
Arthur Rd. BH23 26 A3
Asquith Clo. BH23 26 D4
Auster Clo. BH23 27 G3
Avenue Rd. BH23 26 A2
Avon Bldgs. BH23 26 A2
Avon Rd East. BH23 26 A2
Avon Run Rd. BH23 27 G5
Avon Run Rd. BH23 27 G5
Avon Wharf. BH23 26 C4
Baldwin Clo. BH23 26 D4
Bank Clo. BH23 26 B4
Bargates. BH23 26 A3
Baring Rd. BH6 26 A6
Barrack Rd. BH23 26 A3
Batten Clo. BH23 26 D3
Beaconsfield Rd. BH23 27 H3
Beaufort Clo. BH23 27 H3
Belfield Rd. BH6 26 A6
Bellflower Clo. BH23 27 G2
Belvedere Rd. BH23 26 A3
Beresford Gdns. BH23 27 E4
Bingham Clo. BH23 27 E3
Bingham Rd. BH23 26 D3
Blackberry La. BH23 27 E4
Blenheim Dri. BH23 27 G3
Bluebell Clo. BH23 27 H2
Bodowen Clo. BH23 26 D1
Bodowen Rd. BH23 26 D1
Bonington Clo. BH23 27 E2
Brabazon Dri. BH23 27 G3
Braemar Av. BH6 26 A6
Braemar Clo. BH6 26 A6
Branders Clo. BH6 26 A5
Branders La. BH6 26 A5
Branwell Clo. BH23 26 A1
Briar Clo. BH23 27 E4
Bridge St. BH23 26 C4
Britannia Way. BH23 27 G3
Broadlands Av. BH6 26 A5

Broadway. BH6 26 A6
Bronte Av. BH23 26 A1
Brook Way. BH23 27 H3
Bub La. BH23 27 E4
Buccaneers Clo. BH23 26 D4
Burdock Clo. BH23 27 H1
Bure Clo. BH23 27 H4
Bure Haven Dri. BH23 27 F4
Bure Homage Gdns. BH23 27 G4
Bure Homage La. BH23 27 G4
Bure La. BH23 27 G5
Bure Park. BH23 27 H4
Bure Rd. BH23 27 H4
Burton Clo. BH23 26 D3
Burton Rd. BH23 27 E1
Buttercup Dri. BH23 27 H1
Caledonian Clo. BH23 27 H3
Cameron Rd. BH23 26 D3
Campion Gro. BH23 27 E4
Capesthorne. BH23 27 G5
Caroline Av. BH23 27 E4
Carradale. BH23 27 H2
Castle St. BH23 26 B4
Catalina Clo. BH23 27 G4
Caxton Clo. BH23 27 F3
Celandine Clo. BH23 27 H2
Chant Clo. BH23 26 D3
Charles Rd. BH23 27 F2
Charlotte Clo. BH23 27 G4
Chichester Way. BH23 27 G5
Christchurch
  By-Pass. BH23 26 B3
Church La. BH23 26 B4
Church St. BH23 26 B4
Clarendon Rd. BH23 26 A3
Clematis Clo. BH23 27 H1
Cliff Dri. BH23 27 H4
Clover Clo. BH23 27 H2
Coast Guard Way. BH23 27 E5
Colbridge Grn. BH23 26 D4
Columbine Clo. BH23 27 H1
Comet Way. BH23 27 G3
Convent Wk. BH23 26 B5
Cornflower Dri. BH23 27 H1
Court Clo. BH23 26 D3
Creedy Path. BH23 26 B4
Cricket Clo. BH23 27 F5
Cringle Av. BH6 26 A5
Croft Rd. BH23 27 F3
Cunningham Clo. BH23 27 F4
Curlew Rd. BH23 27 F4
Dairy Clo. BH23 26 D3
Dakota Way. BH23 27 G3
Dehavilland Way. BH23 27 F5
Delft Mews. BH23 26 C4
Delta Clo. BH23 27 G3
Dennistoun Av. BH23 27 E3
Disraeli Rd. BH23 26 D4
Donnington Dri. BH23 27 H3
Dorset Rd. BH23 27 E2
Douglas Av. BH23 26 A4
Drake Clo. BH23 27 F4
Draper Rd. BH23 27 E3
Druitt Rd. BH23 27 E2
Ducking Stool La. BH23 26 B4
Duncliff Rd. BH6 26 A6
Dunlin Clo. BH23 27 G5
Edward Rd. BH23 27 F2
Elderberry La. BH23 27 F4
Emily Clo. BH23 26 A1
Everest Rd. BH23 26 D2
Fairfield. BH23 26 B3
Fairmile Rd. BH23 26 A1
Fairway Dri. BH23 26 A4
Falcon Dri. BH23 27 F5
Farm La. BH23 27 F5
Fishermans Bank. BH23 27 E5
Flambard Av. BH23 26 A1
Fountain Way. BH23 26 B4
Foxglove Clo. BH23 27 H2
Foxwood Av. BH23 27 H2
Friars Rd. BH23 26 B4
Frobisher Clo. BH23 27 F4
Fulmar Rd. BH23 27 G5
Gladstone Rd. BH23 26 D4
Gleadowe Av. BH23 26 A3
Glendale Rd. BH23 26 A6
Glengarry Way. BH23 26 C1
Gordon Way. BH23 26 C1
Grafton Clo. BH23 26 A3
Grange Rd. BH23 27 G3
Grebe Clo. BH23 27 F4
Green Acres. BH23 27 F4
Grove Rd East. BH23 26 A2
Groveley Rd. BH23 27 E4
Haarlem Mews. BH23 26 C3

Haking Clo. BH23 26 D3
Halifax Way. BH23 27 G3
Hamilton Clo. BH23 27 E5
Harbour Cres. BH23 27 E5
Harbour Rd. BH6 26 B6
Hardy Clo. BH23 27 F5
Harland Rd. BH6 26 A6
Hawkins Clo. BH23 27 F4
Haworth Clo. BH23 26 A1
Hawthorn Rd. BH23 27 E2
High St. BH23 26 B4
Highcliffe Rd. BH23 27 G2
Hillary Rd. BH23 27 E2
Hoburne La. BH23 27 H1
Holly Gdns. BH23 26 D1
Honeybourne Cres.
  BH23 26 A6
Honeysuckle Way.
  BH23 27 G2
Howard Clo. BH23 27 F4
Howe Clo. BH23 27 F5
Hunt Rd. BH23 27 E2
Hunter Clo. BH23 27 G3
Hynesbury Rd. BH23 27 H4
INDUSTRIAL ESTATES:
  Priory Ind Park. BH23 27 G3
Inveravon. BH23 27 F5
Irvine Way. BH23 27 E2
Island View Av. BH23 27 G4
Jellicoe Clo. BH23 27 F4
Johnstone Rd. BH23 27 E4
Kestrel Dri. BH23 27 G4
Keyes Clo. BH23 27 F4
Kingfisher Way. BH23 27 F5
Kings Av. BH23 26 A4
Kingsley Av. BH6 26 A6
Kingsley Clo. BH6 26 A2
Knapp Clo. BH23 26 A2
Knapp Mill Av. BH23 26 A2
Knowles Clo. BH23 26 D3
Ladysmith Clo. BH23 26 D3
Lancaster Clo. BH23 27 H3
Lark Rd. BH23 27 G4
Latch Farm Av. BH23 26 A2
Le Patourel Clo. BH23 26 D3
Ledbury Rd. BH23 27 E5
Leyside. BH23 27 F4
Lineside. BH23 26 C1
Lingwood Av. BH23 27 E4
Livingstone Rd. BH23 26 D3
Lyndhurst Rd. BH23 27 G2
Lysander Clo. BH23 27 H3
Magdalen La. BH23 26 A4
Magnolia Clo. BH6 26 A5
Mallard Clo. BH23 27 F4
Mallory Clo. BH23 27 F2
Manor Rd. BH23 26 A4
Marabout Clo. BH23 26 D3
*Marina Vw,
  Willow Way. BH23 26 A5
Marmion Grn. BH23 27 E3
Marsh Ditch. BH23 26 A4
Marsh La. BH23 26 D4
Martins Hill Clo. BH23 26 C1
Martins Hill La. BH23 26 C1
Masterson Clo. BH23 26 D3
Meadowland. BH23 27 E4
Medina Way. BH23 27 H4
Medlar Clo. BH23 26 D1
Meredith Clo. BH23 27 H4
Merlin Way. BH23 27 G5
Mill Rd. BH23 26 A2
Miller Rd. BH23 26 D3
Millhams St. BH23 26 B4
Minterne Rd. BH23 27 E4
Moffat Rd. BH23 26 D3
Monkshood Clo. BH23 27 H1
Monkswell Grn. BH23 26 C4
Mortimer Clo. BH23 27 G4
Mountbatten Clo. BH23 27 F5
Mude Gdns. BH23 27 F5
Mudeford. BH23 27 E5
Mudeford Green Clo.
  BH23 27 F5
Mudeford La. BH23 27 E4
Nelson Dri. BH23 27 F4
Newcroft Gdns. BH23 26 A2
Newlands Rd. BH23 27 F3
Normandy Dri. BH23 26 D3
Normandy Rd. BH23 27 E1
Norton Clo. BH23 26 D3
Nugent Rd. BH6 26 A6
Orchard Clo. BH23 26 A4
Orchid Way. BH23 26 C3
Osprey Clo. BH23 27 F5
Palmerston Av. BH23 26 D4
Park Gdns. BH23 27 E3

Partridge Clo. BH23 27 F5
Pauntley Rd. BH23 27 E4
Pelham Clo. BH23 26 D4
Peregrine Rd. BH23 27 F4
Pinehurst Av. BH23 27 F5
Pipers Dri. BH23 27 G3
Poppy Clo. BH23 27 H2
Portfield Clo. BH23 26 A2
Portfield Rd. BH23 26 A3
Primrose Way. BH23 27 H1
Princess Av. BH23 26 B4
Priory Ct. BH23 26 B4
Priory Quay. BH23 26 B5
Promenade. BH23 27 H5
Purewell. BH23 26 C4
Purewell Cross Rd.
  BH23 26 C3
Purewell Lodge. BH23 26 D4
Quay Rd. BH23 26 B4
Queens Av. BH23 26 B5
Queens Rd. BH23 26 D4
Raleigh Clo. BH23 27 F5
Raven Way. BH23 27 G5
Redvers Rd. BH23 27 E3
Regent Way. BH23 26 B4
Reid St. BH23 26 A3
Ricardo Cres. BH23 27 G4
Riverdale La. BH23 26 A4
*Riverlea Mews,.
  Marsh La. BH23 26 D4
Riverlea Rd. BH23 26 A4
Riversdale Rd. BH6 26 A6
Robins Way. BH23 27 G5
Rodney Dri. BH23 27 F4
Roeshot Hill. BH23 27 H1
Rolls Dri. BH6 26 B6
Roscrea Clo. BH6 26 B6
Roscrea Dri. BH6 26 B6
Rosedale Clo. BH23 27 E4
Rotterdam Dri. BH23 26 C3
Rushford Warren. BH23 27 E5
Russell Dri. BH23 27 E4
Saffron Dri. BH23 27 H2
St Johns Rd. BH23 26 A4
St Margarets Av. BH23 26 A4
Salisbury Rd. BH23 26 A4
Sandown Rd. BH23 27 E4
Sandy Plot. BH23 26 C1
Sarah Sands Clo. BH23 26 D2
Saxon Sq. BH23 26 B4
Saxonford Rd. BH23 27 H3
Scotts Grn. BH23 27 F2
Scotts Hills La. BH23 26 D3
Seafield Rd. BH23 27 H4
Seaway Av. BH23 27 H3
Sheldrake Rd. BH23 27 G5
Shorts Clo. BH23 26 C1
Silver St. BH23 26 B4
Slinn Rd. BH23 26 D3
Snowdrop Gdns. BH23 27 H1
Somerford Av. BH23 27 G2
Somerford Rd. BH23 27 E3
Somerford Way. BH23 27 E3
Sopers La. BH23 26 A4
Sopwith Clo. BH23 27 G4
Sorrell Way. BH23 27 G2
South View Rd. BH23 26 A4
Southcliffe Rd. BH23 27 H4
Southey Rd. BH23 27 E2
Speedwell Dri. BH23 27 G2
Springfield Av. BH6 26 A6
*Staniforth Ct,
  Stony La BH23. 26 C4
Stanpit. BH23 26 C4
Station Rd. BH23 26 A3
Stirling Way. BH23 27 G4
Stony La. BH23 26 C1
Stony Lane Sth. BH23 26 C4
Stour Rd. BH23 26 A4
Stourbank Rd. BH23 26 A4
Strete Mnt. BH23 27 E3
Stroud Gdns. BH23 27 E4
Stroud La. BH23 27 E4
Stroud Park Av. BH23 27 E3
Summers La. BH23 26 D1
Sunderland Dri. BH23 27 H3
Swordfish Dri. BH23 27 G3
Tangmere Clo. BH23 27 G4
Tensing Rd. BH23 26 D2
The Buttery. BH23 26 D3
The Coppice. BH23 27 G4
The Hawthorns. BH23 27 E4
*The Moorings,
  Willow Way. BH23 26 A5
The Runway. BH23 27 H4
Thornbury Rd. BH6 26 A6

Tilburg Rd. BH23 26 C3
Treebys Clo. BH23 26 D1
Trefoil Way. BH23 27 H2
Troak Clo. BH23 26 D2
Twynham Av. BH23 26 A3
Utrecht Clo. BH23 26 C3
Vecta Clo. BH23 27 H4
Verwood Cres. BH6 26 A6
Vetch Clo. BH23 27 H2
Vickery Way. BH23 26 D2
Victoria Rd. BH23 27 E5
Viking Clo. BH23 26 A6
Viking Way,
  Mudeford. BH23 27 G5
Viking Way, Wick. BH6 26 A6
Villette Clo. BH23 26 A1
Viscount Dri. BH23 27 G3
Vulcan Way. BH23 27 G3
Walcott Av. BH23 26 A1
Warren Av. BH23 27 F5
Water Mill Rd. BH23 26 A2
Waterside. BH23 27 E6
Watery La. BH23 27 F1
Wellesley Av. BH23 27 H3
Wessex Clo. BH23 27 H3
West View Rd. BH23 26 D4
Westfield Gdns. BH23 27 G1
Whitehall. BH23 26 B4
Whitehayes Rd. BH23 26 C1
Wick La,
  Christchurch. BH23 26 B4
Wick La, Wick. BH6 26 A5
Wickfield Av. BH23 26 B4
Wickfield Clo. BH23 26 B4
Wicklea Rd. BH6 26 B6
Wickmeads Rd. BH6 26 A5
Wildfell Clo. BH23 26 A1
Wildown Rd. BH6 26 A6
Willow Dri. BH6 26 A5
Willow Way. BH6 26 A5
Wilverley Rd. BH23 27 F3
Wolfe Clo. BH23 26 D3
Wren Clo. BH23 27 G5
Yarrow Clo. BH23 27 H2

CORFE CASTLE

Abbotts Cotts. BH20 24 B5
Battlemead. BH20 24 C5
Calcraft Rd. BH20 24 C5
Colletts Clo. BH20 24 C6
East St. BH20 24 B4
Halves Cotts. BH20 24 B6
Higher Filbank. BH20 24 C5
Higher Gdns. BH20 24 C5
Hollands Clo. BH20 24 B5
Market Sq. BH20 24 B4
Mead Rd. BH20 24 C6
Mohune Way. BH20 24 C4
Sandy Hill La. BH20 24 C4
Springwell Clo. BH20 24 B5
The Bindells. BH20 24 C3
The Dollings. BH20 24 C6
Tilbury Mead. BH20 24 C6
Townsend Mead. BH20 24 C6
Townsend Rd. BH20 24 C6
Webbers Clo. BH20 24 B5
West St. BH20 24 B4

CORFE MULLEN

Abbotsbury Rd. BH18 25 E2
Albert Rd. BH21 25 C2
Amber Rd. BH21 25 B3
Anvil Cres. BH18 25 E2
Ascot Rd. BH18 25 F3
Barry Gdns. BH18 25 F2
Barters La. BH18 25 E4
Beacon Gdns. BH18 25 D4
Beacon Hill La. BH21 25 A4
Beacon Rd. BH18 25 D4
Beacon Way. BH18 25 D4
Beech Clo. BH18 25 D3
Beechbank Av. BH18 Inset
Birch Clo. BH18 25 C1
Blacksmith Clo. BH21 25 C2
Blaney Way. BH21 25 C1
Blythe Rd. BH21 25 C1
Bognor Rd. BH18 25 F3
Broadmoor Rd. BH21 25 B1
Broadstone Way. BH18 25 F4
Brook La. BH21 25 B1
Brownsea Av. BH21 25 D1

Drake Rd. BH15 36 C6
East Quay Rd. BH15 36 C6
East St. BH15 36 C5
Elizabeth Rd. BH15 36 C4
Emerson Clo. BH15 36 C5
Emerson Rd. BH15 36 C5
Enfield Rd. BH15 36 D1
Falkland Sq. BH15 36 C5
Fernside Rd. BH15 36 D2
Ferry Rd. BH15 36 B6
Fishermans Rd. BH15 36 C6
Fleets Lane. BH15 36 B1
Furnell Rd. BH15 36 D6
Garland Rd. BH15 36 D3
Globe La. BH15 36 C5
Green Clo. BH15 36 C5
Green Gdns. BH15 36 C6
Green Rd. BH15 36 C5
Harbour Hill Cres. BH15 36 D2
Haynes Av. BH15 36 C3
Heath Av. BH15 36 C1
Heckford Rd. BH15 36 C5
Hennings Pk Rd. BH15 36 D2
High St. BH15 36 B6
Hiley Rd. BH15 36 C1
Hill St. BH15 36 B5
Holes Bay Rd. BH15 36 A1
Ivor Rd. BH15 36 A6
Jolliffe Av. BH15 36 D3
Jolliffe Rd. BH15 36 D3
Kingland Cres. BH15 36 C5
Kingland Rd. BH15 36 C4
Kingsbere Rd. BH15 36 D2
Kingston Rd. BH15 36 D3
Labrador Dri. BH15 36 D6
Lagland St. BH15 36 C5
Lander Clo. BH15 36 D6
Levets La. BH15 36 B5
Longfleet Rd. BH15 36 D4
Maple Rd. BH15 36 D4
Market St. BH15 36 B5
Market St. BH15 36 B5
Marlott Rd. BH15 36 C2
Marnhull Rd. BH15 36 D3
Marston Rd. BH15 36 B5
Mellstock Rd. BH15 36 C2
Middle Rd. BH15 36 D1
Milestone Rd. BH15 36 C1
Mount Pleasant Rd. BH15 36 D4
Nansen Av. BH15 36 C3
New Harbour Rd. BH15 36 B6
New Harbour Rd West. BH15 36 A6
New Orchard. BH15 36 B5
New Quay Rd. BH15 36 A6
New St. BH15 36 B5
Newfoundland Dri. BH15 36 D5
North St. BH15 36 C5
Oakdale Rd. BH15 36 D1
Oakfield Rd. BH15 36 C1
Old Orchard. BH15 36 B5
Palmer Rd. BH15 36 C2
Paradise St. BH15 36 B6
Parish Rd. BH15 36 D4
Park Lake Rd. BH15 36 D5
Parkstone Rd. BH15 36 D4
Perry Gdns. BH15 36 C6
Pitwines Clo. BH15 36 C5
Popes Rd. BH15 36 D1
Pound La. BH15 36 D2
Preston Rd. BH15 36 C1
Prosperous St. BH15 36 C5
Rectory Rd. BH15 36 B1
Rigler Rd. BH15 36 A5
Rowland Av. BH15 36 D1
St Aubyns Ct. BH15 36 B5
St James's Clo. BH15 36 B5
St Johns Rd. BH15 36 D3
St Margarets Rd. BH15 36 D4
St Marys Rd. BH15 36 D4
Sandbourne Rd. BH15 36 D3
Sandpit La. BH15 36 D4
Sarum St. BH15 36 D4
Seldown. BH15 36 D5
Seldown Bridge. BH15 36 D5
Seldown La. BH15 36 C4
Seldown Rd. BH15 36 D4
Seliot Clo. BH15 36 C4
Serpentine La S. BH15 36 C4
Serpentine Rd. BH15 36 C4
Shaftesbury Rd. BH15 36 D4
Shapwick Rd. BH15 36 A6
Sherrin Clo. BH15 36 D2
Shottsford Rd. BH15 36 C2
Simmonds Clo. BH15 36 D2

Skinner St. BH15 36 C6
Slip Way. BH15 36 B5
Somerby Rd. BH15 36 D1
South Rd. BH15 36 C5
Stanley Green Cres. BH15 36 B2
Stanley Green Rd. BH15 36 B2
Stanley Rd. BH15 36 C5
Staple Close La. BH15 36 C1
Station Rd. BH15 36 A6
Stenhurst Rd. BH15 36 D1
Sterte Av. BH15 36 B3
Sterte Av West. BH15 36 B3
Sterte Clo. BH15 36 B3
Sterte Esp. BH15 36 C4
Sterte Rd. BH15 36 C4
Stokes Av. BH15 36 C3
Strand St. BH15 36 B6
Tatnam La. BH15 36 C3
Tatnam Rd. BH15 36 C3
Taverner Clo. BH15 36 B5
Thames Alley. BH15 36 B6
Thames St. BH15 36 B6
The Quay. BH15 36 B6
Towngate Bridge. BH15 36 C5
Vallis Clo. BH15 36 C6
Vicarage Rd. BH15 36 C1
Waldren Clo. BH15 36 D5
Waverley Cres. BH15 36 C1
Well La. BH15 36 C2
West Quay Rd. BH15 36 B5
West St. BH15 36 B5
West View Rd. BH15 36 C3
Westons La. BH15 36 C5
Whatleigh Clo. BH15 36 C5
White Horse Dri. BH15 36 C2
Whittles Way. BH15 36 B5
Wilkins Way. BH15 36 B5
Willis Way. BH15 36 B1
Wimborne Rd. BH15 36 C1
Wingfield Av. BH15 36 D1
Winifred Rd. BH15 36 D1
Winterbourne Clo. BH15 36 D2
Winterbourne Rd. BH15 36 D2

PRESTON

Barton Dri. DT3 37 A3
Baydon Clo. DT3 37 B3
Bridge Inn Rd. DT3 37 C2
Brookmead Clo. DT3 37 C1
Brookside Clo. DT3 37 B3
Brunel Dri. DT3 37 B2
Cedar Dri. DT3 37 B3
Chalbury Clo. DT3 37 A3
Church Rd. DT3 37 C3
Churchward Av. DT3 37 B2
Collet Clo. DT3 37 B2
Coombe Valley Rd. DT3 37 A1
Cornhill Way. DT3 37 C1
Fir Dri. DT3 37 B3
Fisherbridge Rd. DT3 37 C3
Halstock Clo. DT3 37 B3
Hambro Ter. DT3 37 C2
Hawksworth Clo. DT3 37 B3
Holcombe Clo. DT3 37 C3
Horyford Clo. DT3 37 C3
Littlemoor Rd. DT3 37 A3
Marley Clo. DT3 37 B2
Maunsell Av. DT3 37 B3
Mawdywalls. DT3 37 C2
Medway Dri. DT3 37 A3
Mill La. DT3 37 C2
Millers Clo. DT3 37 C2
Mission Hall La. DT3 37 C1
Moorcombe Dri. DT3 37 A3
Old Bincombe La. DT3 37 C1
Old Granary Clo. DT3 37 B2
Plaisters La. DT3 37 C1
Preston Rd. DT3 37 A3
Puddledock La. DT3 37 B2
Reynards Way. DT3 37 C2
Rhosewood Dri. DT3 37 A2
Rimbrow Clo. DT3 37 B2
Rymbury. DT3 37 C2
Seven Acres Rd. DT3 37 B2
Silver St. DT3 37 C1
Stanier Rd. DT3 37 B2
Stroudley Cres. DT3 37 B2
Sunnyfields. DT3 37 B2
Sutton Clo. DT3 37 C1
Sutton Court Lawns. DT3 37 C1
Sutton Pk. DT3 37 C2
Sutton Rd. DT3 37 C2

Telford Clo. DT3 37 B3
The Wier. DT3 37 C2
Verlands Rd. DT3 37 C2
Wainwright Clo. DT3 37 B2
White Horse Dri. DT3 37 C2
White Horse La. DT3 37 C1
Willow Cres. DT3 37 B3
Winslow Rd. DT3 37 C2

PUDDLETOWN

Ash Tree Clo. DT2 37 C6
Athelhampton Rd. DT2 37 C6
Beech Rd. DT2 37 C6
Bellbury Clo. DT2 37 C5
Brymer Rd. DT2 37 C6
Butt Clo. DT2 37 C6
Charminster La. DT2 37 A5
Chine Hill La. DT2 37 A4
Cobbs Pl. DT2 37 C6
Coombe Rd. DT2 37 B6
Druce La. DT2 37 B4
High St. DT2 37 B5
Kingsmead. DT2 37 B5
Mill St. DT2 37 C5
Millom La. DT2 37 C6
New St. DT2 37 B6
Rod Hill La. DT2 37 C5
Styles La. DT2 37 B5
The Green. DT2 37 C5
The Moor. DT2 37 B5
The Square. DT2 37 C5
Thompson Clo. DT2 37 B4
Walpole St. DT2 37 C5
White Hill. DT2 37 B6
Willoughby Clo. DT2 37 B6

SHAFTESBURY

Abbey Clo. SP7 38 C3
Abbey Walk. SP7 38 C3
Angel La. SP7 38 C2
Ash Clo. SP7 38 D1
Barton Clo. SP7 38 C2
Barton Hill. SP7 38 C2
Beaufoy Clo. SP7 38 E2
Bell St. SP7 38 C2
Belmont Clo. SP7 38 D3
Bimport. SP7 38 B3
Blackmore Rd. SP7 38 E1
Bleke St. SP7 38 C2
Boundary Rd. SP7 38 D3
Boyne Mead. SP7 38 D3
Boyne Mead. SP7 38 D3
Breach La. SP7 38 B3
Brinscombe La. SP7 38 D4
Butts Mead. SP7 38 D4
Calves La. SP7 38 A1
Castle Hill Clo. SP7 38 B2
Christys La. SP7 38 D2
Church Hill . SP7 38 A2
Church Walk. SP7 38 C3
Coppice St. SP7 38 D2
Cranbourne Dri. SP7 38 D1
Crookhays. SP7 38 D1
Dark La. SP7 38 C2
Fairlane. SP7 38 E3
Fountains Mead. SP7 38 C2
Foyle Hill. SP7 38 A4
French Mill Rise. SP7 38 D3
Frenchmill La. SP7 38 D3
Gillingham Rd. SP7 38 A1
Gold Hill. SP7 38 C3
Granville Gdns. SP7 38 C2
Great La. SP7 38 D3
Grosvenor Rd. SP7 38 D1
Haimes La. SP7 38 C2
Hawkesdene. SP7 38 D4
Hawkesdene La. SP7 38 D4
Hawthorne Clo. SP7 38 E1
Heathfields Way. SP7 38 D1
High St. SP7 38 C3
Higher Blandford Rd. SP7 38 E4
Homefield. SP7 38 D1
Horse Ponds. SP7 38 B2
Imber Rd. SP7 38 E2
Jeaneau Clo. SP7 38 D2
Jubilee Path. SP7 38 C3
Kings Hill. SP7 38 C3
Kingsman La. SP7 38 C3
Laneside. SP7 38 D1
Langfords La. SP7 38 B3

Laundry La. SP7 38 B3
Layton La. SP7 38 C3
Linden Park. SP7 38 E3
Lindlar Clo. SP7 38 D2
Little Content La. SP7 38 D2
Little Down. SP7 38 D1
Long Cross. SP7 38 A2
Long Mead. SP7 38 D2
Love La. SP7 38 B3
Lower Blandford Rd. SP7 38 D3
Lyons Walk. SP7 38 C3
Magdalane La. SP7 38 C3
Mampitts La. SP7 38 E3
Mampitts Rd. SP7 38 E3
Maple Clo. SP7 38 D1
Meadow Clo. SP7 38 D1
Motcombe Rd. SP7 38 C1
Mustons La. SP7 38 C2
Nettlebed Nursery. SP7 38 B2
Nettlecombe. SP7 38 E2
New La. SP7 38 F4
New Rd. SP7 38 B2
Old St. SP7 38 D3
Oxencroft. SP7 38 D1
Paddock Clo. SP7 38 E4
Park La. SP7 38 C3
Park Walk. SP7 38 C3
Parsons Pool. SP7 38 C2
Pine Walk. SP7 38 B3
Pix Mead Gdns. SP7 38 E3
Pound La. SP7 38 D3
Raspberry La. SP7 38 B3
Ratcliffs Gdns. SP7 38 B3
Ridgeway. SP7 38 D1
Rowan Clo. SP7 38 E1
Rumbolds Rd. SP7 38 D3
Rutter Clo. SP7 38 E3
St Edwards Clo. SP7 38 D2
St Georges Rd. SP7 38 D3
St James St. SP7 38 B3
St Jamess Common. SP7 38 B4
St Johns Hill. SP7 38 B3
St Lawrences Cres. SP7 38 D1
St Martins La. SP7 38 D3
Salisbury Rd. SP7 38 D3
Salisbury St. SP7 38 B3
Sally Kings La. SP7 38 B2
Saxon Spur. SP7 38 D2
Shaftesbury By-Pass. SP7 38 B2
Shiphouse La. SP7 38 C4
Shooters La. SP7· 38 C3
Snakey La. SP7 38 C3
Spring Field. SP7 38 D1
Stoney Path. SP7 38 B3
Sturminster Rd. SP7 38 B4
Sweetmans Rd. SP7 38 D2
Tanyard La. SP7 38 B3
Ten Acres. SP7 38 E2
The Beeches. SP7 38 C2
The Butts. SP7 38 A2
The Commons. SP7 38 C2
The Knapp. SP7 38 B2
The Venn. SP7 38 D2
Tobys St. SP7 38 C2
Tollgate Park. SP7 38 D1
Tout Hill. SP7 38 B2
Umbers Hill. SP7 38 B3
Victoria St. SP7 38 C2
Watery La. SP7 38 C3
Well La. SP7 38 B2
Westminster Clo. SP7 38 D1
Whitehart La. SP7 38 C3
Wincombe La. SP7 38 D2
Windmill Clo. SP7 38 D1
Woolands La. SP7 38 B2
Yeatmans Clo. SP7 38 B2
Yeatmans La. SP7 38 B2

SHERBORNE

Abbey Clo. DT9 39 D3
Abbey Rd. DT9 39 D3
Abbots Way. DT9 39 A4
Acreman Ct. DT9 39 C2
Acreman Pl. DT9 39 D3
Acreman St. DT9 39 C2
Askwith Clo. DT9 39 A4
Back La. DT9 39 D2
Barton Gdns. DT9 39 B2
Blackberry La. DT9 39 C3
Bradford Rd. DT9 39 A3
Bridewell La. DT9 39 C3

Bristol Rd. DT9 39 D1
Castle Rd. DT9 39 E1
Castle Town Way. DT9 39 E1
Castleton. DT9 39 E2
Castleton Rd. DT9 39 E2
Chandlers. DT9 39 E1
Cheap St. DT9 39 D2
Chrysanthemum Row. DT9 39 E2
Church Pl. DT9 39 D3
Clanfield. DT9 39 A4
Coldharbour. DT9 39 D2
Cooks La. DT9 39 D3
Coombe Rd. DT9 39 B3
Cornhill. DT9 39 C2
Culvers Clo. DT9 39 C3
Digby Rd. DT9 39 D3
Dorchester Rd. DT9 39 C4
Durrant Pl. DT9 39 D1
Earls Clo. DT9 39 E1
East Mill La. DT9 39 E1
Finger La. DT9 39 D1
Fosters. DT9 39 E2
Gainsborough Dri. DT9 39 A
Gainsborough Hill. DT9 39 E
Gas House La. DT9 39 E
George St. DT9 39 D3
Gravel Pits. DT9 39 D
Greenhill. DT9 39 D3
Half Acres. DT9 39 C
Half Moon La. DT9 39 D
Half Moon St. DT9 39 D
Harbour Rd. DT9 39 E
Harbour Way. DT9 39 D
Hardings House La. DT9 39 A
Higher Cheap St. DT9 39 D
Highmore Rd. DT9 39 B
Hill Brow. DT9 39 B
Hill House Clo. DT9 39 E
Honeycombe Rise. DT9 39 B
Horsecastles. DT9 39 C
Horsecastles La. DT9 39 B
Hospital La. DT9 39 D
Hound St. DT9 39 D
Hunts Mead. DT9 39 A
Kings Cres. DT9 39 D
Kings Rd. DT9 39 D
Kitt Hill. DT9 39 C
Langdons. DT9 39 E
Left Ct. DT9 39 B
Lenthay Clo. DT9 39 B
Lenthay Rd. DT9 39 B
Littlefield. DT9 39 B
Long St. DT9 39 D
Lower Acreman St. DT9 39 D
Ludbourne Rd. DT9 39 E
Manor Ct. DT9 39 D
Marston Rd. DT9 39 A
McCreery Rd. DT9 39 D
Midleaze. DT9 39 A
Mulberry Gdns. DT9 39 C
Nethercoombe La. DT9 39 B
New Rd. DT9 39 D
Newell. DT9 39 C
Newland. DT9 39 C
Newland Dri. DT9 39 E
Noake Rd. DT9 39 E
North Rd. DT9 39 C
Oborne Rd. DT9 39 E
Old Farm East & West. DT9 39 C
Ottery La. DT9 39 C
Pageant Dri. DT9 39 D
Pinford La. DT9 39 F
Powys La. DT9 39 F
Priestlands. DT9 39 D
Priestlands La. DT9 39 D
Quarr Dr. DT9 39 D
Quarr La. DT9 39 D
Raleigh Ct. DT9 39 E
Richmond Clo. DT9 39 C
Richmond Grn. DT9 39 C
Richmond Rd. DT9 39 C
Ridgeway. DT9 39 F
St Catherines Cres. DT9 39 F
St Marys Rd. DT9 39 F
St Pauls Clo. DT9 39 E
St Pauls Grn. DT9 39 E
St Swithins Clo. DT9 39 E
St Swithins Rd. DT9 39 E
School La. DT9 39 D
Sheeplands La. DT9 39 E
Simons Rd. DT9 39 C
South Av. DT9 39 C
South Clo. DT9 39 E
South St. DT9 39 E
Springfield Cres. DT9 39 C

station Rd. DT9 39 D3
Stonedene. DT9 39 D1
Swan Yard. DT9 39 D2
he Avenue. DT9 39 E2
he Furlongs. DT9 39 D1
he Green. DT9 39 D2
he Hayes. DT9 39 D3
he Maltings. DT9 39 E3
he Sheeplands. DT9 39 B1
he Wilderness. DT9 39 E3
hornbank Ct. DT9 39 E3
inneys La. DT9 39 E2
rendle St. DT9 39 D3
rent Path La. DT9 39 E2
Jnderown La. DT9 39 F1
Vernalls Rd. DT9 39 D1
Vest Mill La. DT9 39 C4
Vestbridge Pk. DT9 39 B4
Vestbury. DT9 39 C4
Vestfield. DT9 39 B4
Vidforth Clo. DT9 39 A4
Vingfield Rd. DT9 39 C3
Vootton Gro. DT9 39 D1
Vynnes Clo. DT9 39 B3
Vynnes Rise. DT9 39 B3
Yeovil Rd. DT9 39 A3

SHILLINGSTONE
CHILD OKEFORD

llen Clo. DT11 40 C3
pple Acre. DT11 40 C1
ere Marsh. DT11 40 A3
landford Rd. DT11 40 B5
Brodham Way. DT11 40 A6
andys La. DT11 40 C3
halwell. DT11 40 C3
hurch Rd. DT11 40 B5
Cookswell. DT11 40 A4
oombe Rd. DT11 40 B6
uck St. DT11 40 D3
veretts La. DT11 40 B6
old Hill. DT11 40 B1
reenway. DT11 40 C2
reenway La. DT11 40 B2
unn La. DT11 40 B6
ayward La. DT11 40 C2
igh St. DT11 40 B5
line Town La. DT11 40 B5
lolloway La. DT11 40 C6
lomefield. DT11 40 C2
loneysuckle Gdns.
DT11 40 B6
acobs Ladder. DT11 40 C2
napps. DT11 40 A4
notts Clo. DT11 40 C2
anchards. DT11 40 A5
anchards La. DT11 40 A6
ittle La. DT11 40 A4
Jelway Gdns. DT11 40 D3
Jelway La. DT11 40 C3
Jillbrook Clo. DT11 40 C1
Jetmead La. DT11 40 B1
Jutmead Clo. DT11 40 C1
Jlivers Mead. DT11 40 C1
epper Hill. DT11 40 B6
oplar Hill. DT11 40 A5
ortman Dri. DT11 40 C1
uxey La. DT11 40 A6
ectory La. DT11 40 C2
idgeway La. DT11 40 C1
t Nicholas Ct. DT11 40 D2
andy La. DT11 40 D1
chelin Way. DT11 40 B6
haftesbury Rd. DT11 40 C1
hepherds Clo. DT11 40 C2
hillingstone La. DT11 40 A5
outhfield La. DT11 40 B3
pencer Gdns. DT11 40 C6
tation Rd,
Child Okeford. DT11 40 C3
tation Rd,
Shillingstone. DT11 40 A4
tour Clo. DT11 40 C6
he Butts. DT11 40 D3
he Cross,
Child Okeford. DT11 40 C2
he Cross,
Shillingstone. DT11 40 A5
he Hollow. DT11 40 C1
pper Street. DT11 40 D2
Vessex Av. DT11 40 B6

STALBRIDGE

Barrow Hill. DT10 41 A3
Blackmore Rd. DT10 41 C2
Boyle Clo. DT10 41 C2
Cale Clo. DT10 41 D3
Church Hill. DT10 41 B1
Church Walk. DT10 41 A1
Coppern Way. DT10 41 B1
Drews La. DT10 41 B1
Duck La. DT10 41 B1
Duncliffe Clo. DT10 41 D2
Gold St. DT10 41 B2
Grosvenor Rd. DT10 41 B3
Grove La. DT10 41 B2
Grove La Clo. DT10 41 B2
Hardy Cres. DT10 41 C2
High St. DT10 41 B1
Jarvis Clo. DT10 41 C3
Jarvis Way. DT10 41 C3
Lower Rd. DT10 41 C3
Meadow Clo. DT10 41 C2
New Rd. DT10 41 C2
Park Gro. DT10 41 A2
Park Rd. DT10 41 A2
Pound Clo. DT10 41 B3
Raleigh Rd. DT10 41 C3
Ring St. DT10 41 C3
Robinson Heights.
DT10 41 C2
Silk House Barton.
DT10 41 B2
Springfields. DT10 41 D3
Stalbridge Clo. DT10 41 B2
Station Rd. DT10 41 B2
Sturminster Rd. DT10 41 C3
The Hawthorns. DT10 41 D3
Thrift Clo. DT10 41 D3
Vale Rd. DT10 41 C2
Waterlake. DT10 41 C3
Wessex Rd. DT10 41 D3
Wood La. DT10 41 A3

STURMINSTER
NEWTON

Alder Clo. DT10 41 D5
Alder Rd. DT10 41 D4
Badger Way. DT10 41 C4
Barnes Clo. DT10 41 B5
Bath Rd. DT10 41 B5
Bridge St. DT10 41 A6
Brinsley Clo. DT10 41 A4
Brinsley Ct. DT10 41 A5
Brinsley Mead. DT10 41 A5
Butts Pond. DT10 41 C5
Church La. DT10 41 B5
Church St. DT10 41 B5
Church Walk. DT10 41 B6
Denhall Clo. DT10 41 B4
Durrant. DT10 41 A5
Elm Clo. DT10 41 D5
Filbridge Rise. DT10 41 C4
Friars Moor. DT10 41 C5
Gotts Corner. DT10 41 B6
Goughs Clo. DT10 41 A6
Green Clo. DT10 41 B5
Hambledon View. DT10 41 D5
Hanover Clo. DT10 41 B4
Hinton View. DT10 41 C4
Lane-Fox Ter. DT10 41 B5
Lower Rixon. DT10 41 C5
Manston Rd. DT10 41 C5
Market Cross. DT10 41 B5
Penny St. DT10 41 B5
Pitts Orchard. DT10 41 B4
Quarry Clo. DT10 41 C4
Rabin Hill. DT10 41 C4
Ricketts La. DT10 41 A5
Rivers Mead. DT10 41 D4
Rixon Hill. DT10 41 C4
Shortedge. DT10 41 D4
Station Rd. DT10 41 B5
The Row. DT10 41 B5
The Square. DT10 41 B5
West End. DT10 41 A5
White Lane Clo. DT10 41 B4

SWANAGE/
LANGTON
MATRAVERS

Aigburth Rd. BH19 43 E3
Alderbury Clo. BH19 42 D4
Ancaster Rd. BH19 43 E3
Anglebury Av. BH19 43 F2
Anvil Clo. BH19 42 D4
Argyle Rd. BH19 43 F4
Atlantic Rd. BH19 43 F5
Ballard Est. BH19 43 G1
Ballard Lee. BH19 43 G1
Ballard Rd. BH19 43 G1
Ballard Way. BH19 43 G1
Battlegate Footway.
BH19 43 F3
Battlemead. BH19 43 F2
Bay Clo. BH19 43 G1
Bay Cres. BH19 43 G1
Beach Gdns. BH19 43 F3
Bell St. BH19 42 D4
Belle Vue Rd. BH19 43 G5
Belvedere Rd. BH19 43 G5
Benlease Way. BH19 42 D4
Blouchers La. BH19 43 F4
Bon Accord Rd. BH19 43 F5
Bonfields Av. BH19 43 F2
Brickyard La. BH19 43 E1
Broad Rd. BH19 43 G4
Burlington Rd. BH19 43 G2
*Burts Pl,
High St. BH19 43 G4
Casterbridge Clo. BH19 42 D4
Cauldon Av. BH19 43 F3
Cauldon Barn Rd. BH19 43 F2
Cauldon Cres. BH19 43 F2
Cecil Rd. BH19 43 E4
Chapel La. BH19 43 F4
Church Clo. BH19 43 F4
Church Hill. BH19 43 F4
Cliff Av. BH19 43 G2
Clifton Clo. BH19 43 G2
Clifton Rd. BH19 43 G2
Cluny Cres. BH19 43 G4
Commercial Rd. BH19 43 G4
Coombe Hill. BH19 42 B4
Cornwall Rd. BH19 43 F4
Court Hill. BH19 43 F4
Court Rd. BH19 43 F4
Cow La. BH19 43 E4
Cowlease. BH19 43 F4
Crack La. BH19 42 A3
Cranborne Rd. BH19 43 F4
D'Urberville Dri. BH19 43 F2
Darkie La. BH19 43 E1
Days Rd. BH19 42 D4
De Moulham Rd. BH19 43 G2
Drummond Rd. BH19 43 G5
Durlston Rd. BH19 43 G5
Durnford Drove. BH19 42 A5
Durnford Pl. BH19 43 F4
East Gro. BH19 42 A4
Eldon Ter. BH19 43 E4
Exeter Rd. BH19 43 F4
Findlay Pl. BH19 43 E4
Foxhill Clo. BH19 43 E4
Gannetts Pk. BH19 43 F3
Gilbert Rd. BH19 43 F4
Globe Clo. BH19 43 E4
Godlingston La. BH19 42 D2
Gordon Rd. BH19 43 G4
Grosvenor Rd. BH19 43 G5
Gypshayes. BH19 42 A4
Hanbury Rd. BH19 43 F4
Heather Clo. BH19 43 E4
Hendrie Clo. BH19 43 E4
High Cliff Rd. BH19 43 G2
High St, Langton
Matravers. BH19 42 A4
High St,
Swanage. BH19 43 F1
Hill Rd. BH19 43 F1
Hillsea Rd. BH19 43 E4
Hillview Rd. BH19 43 E4
Hoborne Rd. BH19 42 C4
Holmes Rd. BH19 43 E4
Howard Rd. BH19 43 F4
Ilminster Rd. BH19 43 F3
Institute Rd. BH19 43 G4
Jubilee Rd. BH19 43 F4
Kings Rd East. BH19 43 G4
Kings Rd West. BH19 43 G4
Kingswood Clo. BH19 42 D4

Knollsea Clo. BH19 43 G5
Leeson Clo. BH19 42 D4
Lighthouse Rd. BH19 43 G6
Linden Rd. BH19 43 E4
Locarno Rd. BH19 43 F4
Lower Steppes. BH19 42 B4
Manor Rd. BH19 43 G4
Manwell Dri. BH19 43 F5
Manwell Rd. BH19 43 F5
*Manwells La,
High St. BH19 43 F4
Mariners Dri. BH19 43 E4
Marshall Row. BH19 43 G4
*Mermaid Pl,
Station Pl. BH19 43 G4
Moor Rd. BH19 43 F1
Morriston Rd. BH19 43 E4
Mount Pleasant. BH19 42 A4
Mount Pleasant La.
BH19 43 G4
Mount Scars. BH19 43 F5
Newton Manor Clo.
BH19 43 E4
Newton Manor Gdns.
BH19 43 E4
Newton Rise. BH19 43 E4
Newton Rd. BH19 43 G5
North St. BH19 42 A4
Northbrook Rd. BH19 43 F1
Old Malthouse Rd.
BH19 42 A4
Osborne Rd. BH19 43 F4
Osmay Rd. BH19 43 G6
Panorama Rd. BH19 43 E4
Park Rd. BH19 43 F4
*Peveril Heights,
Marshal Row. BH19 43 G4
Peveril Point Rd. BH19 43 H4
Peveril Rd. BH19 43 G5
Plantation Clo. BH19 43 E5
Priests Rd. BH19 43 E4
Priests Way. BH19 42 C5
Princess Rd. BH19 43 E4
Prospect Cres. BH19 43 E3
Purbeck Ter Rd. BH19 43 G5
Purbeck Vw. BH19 43 E4
Quarry Clo. BH19 43 E4
Queens Mead. BH19 43 F4
Queens Rd. BH19 43 F4
Rabling Rd. BH19 43 F3
Redcliff Rd. BH19 43 G1
Rempstone Back Rd.
BH19 43 G3
Rempstone Rd. BH19 43 G3
Richmond Rd. BH19 43 F4
Rough Height. BH19 43 F5
Russell Av. BH19 43 F5
Russell Dri. BH19 43 F5
St Georges Clo. BH19 42 A4
St Vast Rd. BH19 43 G5
Salisbury Rd. BH19 43 G5
Sambourne Clo. BH19 42 D4
Seaward Rd. BH19 43 G2
Sentry Rd. BH19 43 G4
Serrells Mead. BH19 42 B4
Seymer Rd. BH19 43 G4
Shaston Clo. BH19 42 D4
Shirley Clo. BH19 43 E4
Shore Rd. BH19 43 G2
Shottsford Clo. BH19 42 D4
Solent Rd. BH19 43 G6
South Cliff Rd. BH19 43 G6
South Rd. BH19 43 E4
Springfield Rd. BH19 43 F4
Stafford Rd. BH19 43 G4
Station Pl. BH19 43 G4
Station Rd. BH19 43 G4
Steer Rd. BH19 43 E4
Steppes. BH19 42 B4
Steppes Hill. BH19 42 B4
Streche Rd. BH19 43 G1
Sunnydale Rd. BH19 43 G5
Sunridge Clo. BH19 43 G5
Sunshine Walk. BH19 43 F4
Sydenham Rd. BH19 42 C4
Taunton Rd. BH19 43 G4
The Hyde. BH19 42 A4
The Parade. BH19 43 G4
Three Acre La. BH19 42 B4
Toms Field. BH19 42 A4
*Town Hall La,
Kings Rd East. BH19 43 G4
Townsend Rd. BH19 43 F4
Ulwell Rd. BH19 43 F1
Valley Rd. BH19 42 B3
Victoria Av. BH19 43 E3
Victoria Rd. BH19 43 G2

*Victoria Ter,
Jubilee Rd. BH19 42 D4
Vivian Pk. BH19 43 F2
Walrond Rd. BH19 43 F3
Washpond La, Langton
Matravers. BH19 42 D2
Washpond La,
New Swanage. BH19 43 E1
*Wessex Ct, De
Moulham Rd. BH19 43 G2
Wessex Way. BH19 43 F2
West Dri. BH19 43 G4
West Durlston La. BH19 43 G5
Whitecliff Rd. BH19 43 F1
Wills Rd. BH19 43 E4
*Wilson Ct,
Durnford Pl. BH19 43 F4
York Ter. BH19 43 G4

UPWEY
BROADWEY

Beech Rd. DT3 47 B5
Beverley Rd. DT3 47 D6
Blackberry La. DT3 47 C6
Brambling Clo. DT3 47 D5
Bridlebank Way. DT3 47 C5
Broadwey Clo. DT3 47 C5
Brookton La. DT3 47 C6
Camedown Clo. DT3 47 C6
Chaffinch Clo. DT3 47 D6
Chapel La. DT3 47 C4
Church St. DT3 47 A2
Clatton Clo. DT3 47 D6
Coppice Ct. DT3 47 C5
Dorchester Rd. DT3 47 B6
Elwell St. DT3 47 B3
Fieldfare Clo. DT3 47 D6
Firecrest Clo. DT3 47 C5
Friar Waddon La. DT3 47 A1
Georgian Clo. DT3 47 C5
Goldcrest Clo. DT3 47 D5
Goulds Hill. DT3 47 A1
Icen La. DT3 47 C5
Jenner Way. DT3 47 D6
Jestys Av. DT3 47 C5
Jordan Way. DT3 47 C5
Juniper Way. DT3 47 C5
Kestrel Vw. DT3 47 D6
Laurel La. DT3 47 C3
Linnet Clo. DT3 47 C5
Little Mead. DT3 47 B6
Littlemoor Rd. DT3 47 B5
Lorton La. DT3 47 C6
Louviers Rd. DT3 47 D6
Meadow View Rd. DT3 47 C5
Meredin Clo. DT3 47 C5
Mill St. DT3 47 B5
Nightingale Dri. DT3 47 C5
North Merlin Av. DT3 47 B6
Nuthatch Clo. DT3 47 D6
Old Roman Rd. DT3 47 C2
Old Station Rd. DT3 47 C5
Pemberton Clo. DT3 47 C5
Pipit Clo. DT3 47 D6
Prospect Pl. DT3 47 C3
Redpoll Clo. DT3 47 D6
Reedlings Clo. DT3 47 C5
Regency Dri. DT3 47 C2
Ridgeway. DT3 47 C3
Ridgeway Hill. DT3 47 C3
Robin Clo. DT3 47 C5
Rockhampton Clo. DT3 47 C6
St Helier Rd. DT3 47 C6
St Julien Cres. DT3 47 B6
St Lawrence Rd. DT3 47 C4
Sanderling Clo. DT3 47 C5
Selwyn Clo. DT3 47 C4
Shortlands Rd. DT3 47 C4
South Merlin Av. DT3 47 B6
Springfield Clo. DT3 47 C5
Springfield. DT3 47 B6
Stonechat Clo. DT3 47 C5
Stottingway St. DT3 47 C4
The Doves. DT3 47 D6
The Finches. DT3 47 C5
The Orchard. DT3 47 B6
The Woodpeckers. DT3 47 D5
Thurnstone Clo. DT3 47 D6
Victoria Av. DT3 47 C4
Watery La. DT3 47 B5
Westlake Rd. DT3 47 C5
Weyview Cres. DT3 47 B5
Wheatear Clo. DT3 47 C5
Windsor Rd. DT3 47 C5

VERWOOD

Acacia Av. BH31 44 F3
Aggis Farm Rd. BH31 44 B1
Aspen Dri. BH31 44 E2
Badger Way. BH31 44 C3
Bakers Farm Rd. BH31 44 B1
Barberry Way. BH31 44 F3
Beech Clo. BH31 44 B3
Belmont Clo. BH31 44 D3
Berkeley Clo. BH31 44 B1
Bessemer Clo. BH31 44 F4
Bingham Clo. BH31 44 E3
Bingham Dri. BH31 44 D4
Bingham Rd. BH31 44 D4
Bitterne Way. BH31 44 D3
Black Hill. BH31 44 D2
Blackmoor Rd. BH31 44 F3
Blackthorn Way. BH31 44 E3
Bridleways. BH31 44 B2
Bridport Rd. BH31 44 C2
Brook Dri. BH31 44 E3
Brunel Clo. BH31 44 F4
Bugdens La. BH31 44 D2
Burley Clo. BH31 44 B2
Burn Clo. BH31 44 E3
Burnbake Rd. BH31 44 C2
Caradon Pl. BH31 44 A1
Carne Dri. BH31 44 B1
Cartref Clo. BH31 44 C2
Chestnut Clo. BH31 44 E3
Chiltern Dri. BH31 44 C2
Church Hill. BH31 44 B2
Churchfield. BH31 44 B2
Claylake Dri. BH31 44 D3
Coniston Clo. BH31 44 B3
Copse La. BH31 44 C1
Coronation Rd. BH31 44 C1
Cotswold Clo. BH31 44 C2
Crescent Rd. BH31 44 D2
Does La. BH31 44 A2
Dewlands Rd. BH31 44 A2
Dewlands Way. BH31 44 B2
Eastworth Rd. BH31 44 B1
Edmondsham Rd. BH31 44 C1
Enterprise Park. BH31 44 F3
Fairwood Rd. BH31 44 F3
Firs Glen Rd. BH31 44 C3
Forge La. BH31 44 A3
Foxes Clo. BH31 44 C3
Foxhills. BH31 44 E2
Glenwood Rd. BH31 44 C3
Hayward Cres. BH31 44 B2
Hayward Farm Clo. BH31 44 B3
Hayward Way. BH31 44 B2
Hazelwood Dri. BH31 44 E3
Hillside Rd. BH31 44 C1
Holly Gro. BH31 44 B3
Home Farm Rd. BH31 44 B1
Home Farm Way. BH31 44 B1
Horton Way. BH31 44 A3
Howard Rd. BH31 44 C1
Howe La. BH31 44 B3
INDUSTRIAL ESTATES:
Ebblake Ind Est. BH31 44 F3
Verwood Ind Est. BH31 44 D2
Jessica Av. BH31 44 A1
Keswick Way. BH31 44 B2
Laburnum Clo. BH31 44 F3
Lake Rd. BH31 44 D3
Lancaster Dri. BH31 44 B2
Lavender Clo. BH31 44 F3
Lombardy Clo. BH31 44 E2
Magnolia Clo. BH31 44 F3
Manor Gdns. BH31 44 C1
Manor La. BH31 44 C3
Manor Rd. BH31 44 C1
Manor Way. BH31 44 C1
Margards La. BH31 44 A2
Meadow Gro. BH31 44 E3
Meadow Way. BH31 44 D3
Mendip Rd. BH31 44 C2
Moneyfly Rd. BH31 44 E2
Monmouth Clo. BH31 44 E3
Monmouth Dri. BH31 44 E3
Montrose Clo. BH31 44 C2
Moorlands Rd. BH31 44 C1
Newtown La. BH31 44 C3
Newtown Rd. BH31 44 D2
Nightingale Clo. BH31 44 D3
Noon Gdns. BH31 44 E1
Noon Hill Dri. BH31 44 E1
Noon Hill Rd. BH31 44 E2
Oaklands Clo. BH31 44 B2
Orchard Ct. BH31 44 D3
Otter Clo. BH31 44 D3
Owls Rd. BH31 44 D2
Paddock Gro. BH31 44 D3
Park Dri. BH31 44 B1
Pennine Way. BH31 44 C2
Penrith Clo. BH31 44 B3
Pine View Clo. BH31 44 A1
Pine View Rd. BH31 44 A1
Pine Wk. BH31 44 E3
Potterne Way. BH31 44 D4
Purbeck Dri. BH31 44 C2
Raymond Clo. BH31 44 E2
Redmans Vw. BH31 44 B2
Ringwood Rd. BH31 44 C1
Roseberry Clo. BH31 44 F3
Rowan Dri. BH31 44 E3
St Michaels Clo. BH31 44 C3
St Michaels Rd. BH31 44 C3
St Stephens La. BH31 44 D1
Sandy La. BH31 44 D2
Shard Clo. BH31 44 D2
Sherwood Dri. BH31 44 E1
Sleepbrook Clo. BH31 44 B2
Southernhay Rd. BH31 44 E2
Spring Clo. BH31 44 C3
Springfield Clo. BH31 44 C3
Springfield Rd. BH31 44 C3
Squirrel Walk. BH31 44 C3
Stanley Clo. BH31 44 D2
Station Rd. BH31 44 A1
Strathmore Dri. BH31 44 E1
The Chase. BH31 44 F2
The Curlews. BH31 44 D3
The Forestside. BH31 44 F3
The Grove. BH31 44 D2
The Kingfishers. BH31 44 D3
The Lea. BH31 44 D2
The Oaks. BH31 44 B1
Thorne Clo. BH31 44 B1
Verne Rd. BH31 44 D2
Vicarage Rd. BH31 44 C1
West Clo. BH31 44 A1
Whitebeam Way. BH31 44 E3
Wisteria Dri. BH31 44 F4
Woodlinken Clo. BH31 44 E3
Woodlinken Dri. BH31 44 E3
Woodlinken Way. BH31 44 E3
Woodpecker Clo. BH31 44 C3

WAREHAM

Abbots Quay. BH20 45 B6
Admirals Way. BH20 45 C3
Avon Dri. BH20 45 B3
Barnes Rd. BH20 45 A6
Bells Orchard La. BH20 45 C5
Bere Rd. BH20 45 A3
Bestwall Rd. BH20 45 C5
Bestwell Cres. BH20 45 C6
Bonnets La. BH20 45 B5
Bourne Dri. BH20 45 A3
Brixeys La. BH20 45 B5
Bryn Rd. BH20 45 D1
Burns Rd. BH20 45 A3
Carey Clo. BH20 45 A4
Carey Rd. BH20 45 A4
Carrion La. BH20 45 B5
Causeway Clo. BH20 45 B4
Church Ct. BH20 45 C6
Church Grn. BH20 45 B6
Church La. BH20 45 C6
Church St. BH20 45 C6
*Churchwood Ct, St Michaels Rd. BH20 45 B5
Connigar La. BH20 45 C6
Coopers Clo. BH20 45 B5
Courtenay Clo. BH20 45 C3
Cow La. BH20 45 B5
Daniel Dri. BH20 45 B3
Dollins La. BH20 45 B5
Drax Av. BH20 45 B3
East St. BH20 45 B6
East Walls. BH20 45 C6
Edward Cres. BH20 45 B5
Egdon Rd. BH20 45 A3
Elwood Clo. BH20 45 D1
Encombe Rd. BH20 45 B6
Fairway Dri. BH20 45 A3
Filleul Rd. BH20 45 D1
Folly La. BH20 45 B5
Forest Edge Rd. BH20 45 C2
Frome Rd. BH20 45 A6
Gore Hill. BH20 45 C1
Great Lovent Dri. BH20 45 B2
Hardy Rd. BH20 45 A6
Hobbs Clo. BH20 45 B4
Howards La. BH20 45 B5
INDUSTRIAL ESTATES:
Justin Business Pk. BH20 45 B4
Leanne Business Pk. BH20 45 C4
Ryan Business Pk. BH20 45 C3
Johns Rd. BH20 45 B4
Keysworth Dri. BH20 45 D1
*Knightstons Clo, East St. BH20 45 B6
Mellstock Cres. BH20 45 A4
Middle Bere Dri. BH20 45 A3
Miles Av. BH20 45 D1
Mill La. BH20 45 B5
Mistover Rd. BH20 45 A4
Monmouth Rd. BH20 45 A5
Morden Rd. BH20 45 C1
Moretons La. BH20 45 B5
Mount Pleasant. BH20 45 B5
New St. BH20 45 B6
Norden Dri. BH20 45 A3
North Causeway. BH20 45 B4
North St. BH20 45 B5
North Walls. BH20 45 B5
Northmoor Way. BH20 45 A3
Northport Dri. BH20 45 B3
Pound La. BH20 45 B6
Rodgett Cres. BH20 45 D1
Ropers La. BH20 45 B5
Ryan Clo. BH20 45 B4
St Helens Rd. BH20 45 D1
St Johns Hill. BH20 45 B6
St Martins Clo. BH20 45 B5
St Martins La. BH20 45 B5
St Martins Rd. BH20 45 D1
St Marys Clo. BH20 45 A4
St Michaels Rd. BH20 45 B5
Sandford La. BH20 45 B4
Sandford Rd. BH20 45 B4
Seven Barrows Rd. BH20 45 A3
Shatters Hill. BH20 45 B5
Shaw Dri. BH20 45 C2
Sherford Clo. BH20 45 B3
Sherford Dri. BH20 45 B3
Shirley Rd. BH20 45 A6
South Causeway. BH20 45 B6
South St. BH20 45 B6
Stockley Rd. BH20 45 A3
Stour Dri. BH20 45 B3
Stowell Cres. BH20 45 A6
Streche Rd. BH20 45 B5
Tamlin St. BH20 45 D1
Tanners La. BH20 45 B6
Tantinoby La. BH20 45 B3
Tarrant Rd. BH20 45 B3
The Beeches. BH20 45 D1
The Croft. BH20 45 C5
The Quay. BH20 45 B6
Tinkers La. BH20 45 B5
Trent Dri. BH20 45 A3
*Trinity Clo, Abbots Quay. BH20 45 B6
Trinity La. BH20 45 B6
Tyneham Clo. BH20 45 D1
Walls View Rd. BH20 45 A4
Wareham By-Pass. BH20 45 A5
Wellstead Rd. BH20 45 A3
Wessex Oval. BH20 45 A4
West Mill Cres. BH20 45 A4
West St. BH20 45 B6
West Walls. BH20 45 B5
Westminster Rd. BH20 45 A4
Westport Rd. BH20 45 B6
Willow Way. BH20 45 A3
Worgret Rd. BH20 45 A6
Wyatts La. BH20 45 C6

WEST LULWORTH

Beech Clo. BH20 46 C1
Bindon Clo. BH20 46 C1
Bindon Rd. BH20 46 B2
*Chestnut Ct, Moreys Clo. BH20 46 C2
Church Hill. BH20 46 B1
Farm Rd. BH20 46 C1
Moreys Clo. BH20 46 C2
School La. BH20 46 B1
Shepherds Way. BH20 46 C1
Sunnyside Rd. BH20 46 B2
The Launches. BH20 46 B1
Vale Rd. BH20 46 C1
*West Lulworth Farm, Farm Rd. BH20 46 C1

WEST MOORS

Abbey Rd. BH22 52 C5
Abbotts Way. BH22 52 C6
Arnold Clo. BH22 52 A3
Arnold Rd. BH22 52 A3
Ashurst Rd. BH22 52 A3
Avon Rd. BH22 52 B5
Beaufoys Av. BH22 52 A6
Beechwood Rd. BH22 52 C5
Belle Vue Gro. BH22 52 B4
Birch Gro. BH22 52 A4
Blackfield La. BH22 52 A3
Bond Av. BH22 52 A2
Braeside Rd. BH22 52 B3
Canterbury Clo. BH22 52 B5
Castlemain Ct. BH22 52 A4
Charnwood Clo. BH22 52 A4
Compton Cres. BH22 52 D5
Denewood Copse. BH22 52 A3
Denewood Rd. BH22 52 A2
Edgemoor Rd. BH22 52 D5
Elmhurst Rd. BH22 52 B4
Elmhurst Way. BH22 52 C5
Farm Rd. BH22 52 A4
Ferndown By-Pass. BH22 52 A6
Fernside Rd. BH22 52 B4
Fir Clo. BH22 52 A3
Firs Glen Rd. BH22 52 B4
Forest Rd. BH22 52 B3
Glenwood Clo. BH22 52 A4
Glenwood La. BH22 52 B4
Glenwood Rd. BH22 52 A4
Glenwood Way. BH22 52 A4
Hardy Clo. BH22 52 B5
Hardy Rd. BH22 52 B5
Harrison Way. BH22 52 B3
Hazel Dri. BH22 52 A6
Heatherdown Rd. BH22 52 C5
Heatherdown Way. BH22 52 C5
Heathfield Rd. BH22 52 C5
Heathfield Way. BH22 52 C5
Heston Way. BH22 52 A3
Highfield Rd. BH22 52 A2
Kingfisher Clo. BH22 52 B4
Kings Clo. BH22 52 A5
Knightstone Gro. BH22 52 A4
Maloren Way. BH22 52 C5
Mark La. BH22 52 A3
Martins Dri. BH22 52 A6
Merino Way. BH22 52 B5
Milford Clo. BH22 52 C4
Monks Clo. BH22 52 D6
Moorlands Rise. BH22 52 B3
Moorlands Rd. BH22 52 A4
Moorside Rd. BH22 52 A4
Newcombe Rd. BH22 52 A4
Newmans La. BH22 52 A1
Oakhurst Clo. BH22 52 B4
Oakhurst La. BH22 52 B4
Oakhurst Rd. BH22 52 B5
Pennington Clo. BH22 52 A4
Pennington Cres. BH22 52 A4
Pennington Rd. BH22 52 A4
Pinehurst Rd. BH22 52 A5
Priory Rd. BH22 52 C6
Queens Clo. BH22 52 A5
Richie Pl. BH22 52 A2
Ringwood Rd. BH22 52 C6
Riverside Rd. BH22 52 A3
Sarum Av Nth. BH22 52 A2
Sarum Av Sth. BH22 52 A2
Shaftesbury Clo. BH22 52 B4
Shaftesbury Rd. BH22 52 B4
Shirley Clo. BH22 52 B4
Southdown Way. BH22 52 B5
Southern Av. BH22 52 C5
Spinners Clo. BH22 52 A5
Station Rd. BH22 52 A2
Summercroft Way. BH22 52 B4
Teasel Way. BH22 52 B5
The Avenue. BH22 52 A3
Uplands Clo. BH22 52 C6
Uplands Rd. BH22 52 C6
Weavers Clo. BH22 52 B5
West Moors. BH22 52 A
West Moors Rd. BH22 52 A
Woodside Rd. BH22 52 A
Woolslope Clo. BH22 52 B
Woolslope Gdns. BH22 52 B
Woolslope Rd. BH22 52 A

WEYMOUTH

Abbotsbury Rd. DT4 50 C
Acacia Clo. DT4 48 B
Adelaide Cres. DT4 50 C
Albany Rd. DT4 50 B
*Albert St, Park St. DT4 51 F
Alexandra Gdns. DT4 51 F
Alexandra Rd, Charlestown. DT4 50 A
Alexandra Rd, Weymouth. DT4 48 D
All Saints Rd. DT4 50 B
Allamanda Rd. DT3 49 F
Allberry Gdns. DT3 49 G
Alma Rd. DT4 51 E
Almond Gro. DT4 48 B
Ambleside. DT3 48 B
Appletree Clo. DT3 48 C
Aragon Clo. DT4 50 D
Argyle Rd. DT4 48 D
Arlington. DT4 48 B
Ash Way. DT3 49 G
Ashton Rd. DT4 50 D
Astrid Way. DT4 51 F
Augusta Pl. DT 51 F
Avenue Rd. DT4 48 D
Avocet Clo. DT4 50 C
Barclay Rd. DT4 50 D
Barley Way. DT4 51 F
Barnhaven Clo. DT4 50 D
Barrack Rd. DT4 51 F
Barrow Rise. DT4 50 E
Barton Dri. DT3 49 H
Bath St. DT4 51 F
Bayard Rd. DT3 49 E
Baycliff Rd. DT4 50 D
Baydon Clo. DT3 49 H
Beach Clo. DT4 49 E
Beach View Rd. DT4 50 B
Beachdown Way. DT3 49 F
Beaulieu. DT4 48 B
Beaumont Av. DT4 48 D
Bedford Rd. DT4 50 C
Belfield Clo. DT4 50 D
Belfield Pk Av. DT4 50 C
Belfield Pk Dri. DT4 50 C
Belgrave. DT4 48 E
Belgrave Cotts. DT4 48 D
Belle Vue Rd. DT4 51 E
Belmont St. DT4 51 F
Belvidere. DT4 51 F
Ben Nevis Rd. DT4 50 D
Benville Rd. DT4 50 E
Beverley Rd. DT3 49 E
Bincleaves Rd. DT4 51 E
Bincombe Rise. DT3 49 E
Birch Way. DT3 49 F
Blenheim Rd. DT3 48 C
Bodkin La. DT3 49 C
Bodwell St. DT4 51 E
Bohays Dri. DT4 50 E
Boleyn Cres. DT4 50 D
Bond St. DT4 51 F
Boulton Clo. DT4 50
Bowleaze Coveway. DT3 49 C
Brackendown Av. DT3 49
Bradford Rd. DT4 50 D
Briar Clo. DT4 48 A
Brisbane Rd. DT3 49
Broadlands Rd. DT3 48
Broadmeadow Rd. DT4 50
Broughton Cres. DT4 50
Brownlow St. DT4 51
Brunel Dri. DT3 49
Brunswick Ter. DT4 51
Bryants Rd. DT4 50
Bryn Rd. DT4 50
Buddleia Clo. DT3 49
Budmouth Av. DT3 49
Buxton. DT4 50
Buxton Rd. DT4 50
Caledonian Clo. DT4 48
Cambridge Rd. DT4 50
Camp Rd. DT4 50
Campion Clo. DT4 49

Trinity Ter. DT4 51 F3
*Turton St, Gloucester Mews. DT4 51 F2
Tyneham Clo. DT3 48 B3
Ullswater Cres. DT4 48 B4
Underbarn Wk. DT4 51 E5
Vanguard Av. DT4 50 B3
Verne Clo. DT4 51 E4
Verne Rd. DT4 51 E4
Verne Way. DT4 51 E4
Victoria Rd. DT4 50 C5
Victoria St. DT4 51 F1
Victoria Ter. DT4 51 F1
Viscount Rd. DT4 50 B3
Vulcan Clo. DT4 50 B3
Wainwright Clo. DT3 49 H1
Walker Cres. DT4 50 C6
Walpole St. DT4 51 F1
Wardcliffe Rd. DT4 50 D2
Warren Clo. DT4 50 B2
Waverley Rd. DT4 48 C5
Wellington Ct. DT4 51 F3
Wentworth Clo. DT3 49 E1
Wesley St. DT4 51 F2
Wessex Rd. DT4 50 D2
West Bay Cres. DT4 50 B5
West St. DT4 51 E3
Westbourne Rd. DT4 48 D6
Westdowne Clo. DT4 50 C2
Westerhall Rd. DT4 49 E6
Westham Rd. DT4 51 E2
Westhaven. DT4 50 C2
Westhill Clo. DT4 50 B5
Westhill Rd. DT4 50 B5
Weston Rd. DT4 51 E3
Westwey Rd. DT4 51 E3
Weymouth Bay Av. DT4 48 D5
Weymouth Way. DT4 48 B5
White Cross Dri. DT4 50 D4
Williams Av. DT4 50 C5
Willow Cres. DT3 49 H2
Wilton Dri. DT4 50 D3
Wiltshire Av. DT4 50 C1
Winchester Clo. DT4 50 B1
Windermere Cres. DT4 48 C4
Wingreen Clo. DT3 49 H2
Winton Clo. DT4 48 B5
*Woodperton St, Westham Rd. DT4 51 E2
Wooland Gdns. DT4 50 B4
Wyke Oliver Clo. DT3 49 G2
Wyke Oliver Rd. DT3 49 G2
Wyke Rd. DT4 50 C4
Wyke Sq. DT4 50 B4

WIMBORNE MINSTER

Allen Ct. BH21 53 B3
Allen Rd. BH21 53 C5
Allenview Rd. BH21 53 B3
Ashdene. BH21 53 D4
Avenue Rd. BH21 53 C5
Barnes Cres. BH21 53 D5
Beaucroft La. BH21 53 D3
Beaucroft Rd. BH21 53 D3
Beaufort Dri. BH21 53 C3
Birchdale Rd. BH21 53 D4
Blind La. BH21 53 B3
Boundary Dri. BH21 53 C2
Bourne Court. BH21 53 C4
Bradbury Vw. BH21 53 C3
Broadway Gdns. BH21 53 C5
Brook Rd. BH21 53 D5
Burts Hill. BH21 53 B2
Byron Rd. BH21 53 C3
Cemetery Rd. BH21 53 A3
Chapel La. BH21 53 B3
Charles Keightly Ct. BH21 53 D5
Chaucer Clo. BH21 53 B3
Chene Rd. BH21 53 D4
Cheriton Way. BH21 53 C3
Church St. BH21 53 B4
Churchill Rd. BH21 53 D5
Cobbs Rd. BH21 53 D2
Cooks Row. BH21 53 B4
Coppercourt Leaze. BH21 53 C5
Cornmarket. BH21 53 B4
Courtenay Dri. BH21 53 C3
Cowdrys Fld. BH21 53 B3
Cowgrove Rd. BH21 53 A4
Cranborne Rd. BH21 53 B2
Cranfield Av. BH21 53 C4
Crescent Rd. BH21 53 C5
Cromwell Rd. BH21 53 D5
Crown Mead. BH21 53 B4
Culverhayes Clo. BH21 53 A3
Culverhayes Pl. BH21 53 A3
Culverhayes Rd. BH21 53 A3
Cuthburga Rd. BH21 53 C4
Cuthbury Clo. BH21 53 A4
Cuthbury Gdns. BH21 53 A4
Days Ct. BH21 53 D5
Deans Court La. BH21 53 B4
Deans Gro. BH21 53 C2
Derwent Water Rd. BH21 53 C6
Dogdean. BH21 53 B1
East Borough. BH21 53 B3
East St. BH21 53 B4
Eden Gro. BH21 53 C5
Elizabeth Rd. BH21 53 B3
Ethelbert Rd. BH21 53 C5
Fairfield Rd. BH21 53 D4
Farmers Walk. BH21 53 B3
Flower Ct. BH21 53 C5
Furzehill. BH21 53 B1
Giddylake. BH21 53 C3
Glendale Clo. BH21 53 C3
Gordon Rd. BH21 53 D5
Grammar School La. BH21 53 B4
Green Close La. BH21 53 D4
Greenhays Rise. BH21 53 B4
Greenhill Clo. BH21 53 C2
Greenhill La. BH21 53 D3
Greenhill Rd. BH21 53 D3
Grenville Rd. BH21 53 C5
Grove Rd. BH21 53 C5
Gullivers Ct. BH21 53 B3
Hanham Rd. BH21 53 B4
Hardy Cres. BH21 53 D5
High St. BH21 53 B4
Highland Rd. BH21 53 C3
Highland View Clo. BH21 53 D3
Hornbeam Way. BH21 53 D4
Ingram Walk. BH21 53 C5
Julians Rd. BH21 53 A4
King St. BH21 53 B4
Knobcrook Rd. BH21 53 B3
Lacy Clo. BH21 53 C3
Lacy Dri. BH21 53 C3
Legg La. BH21 53 C4
Leigh Gdns. BH21 53 D5
Leigh Rd. BH21 53 C4
Lewens Clo. BH21 53 C4
Lewens La. BH21 53 C4
Livingstone Rd. BH21 53 D5
Long La. BH21 53 D1
Market Way. BH21 53 C5
Marlborough Pl. BH21 53 C3
Melverley Gdns. BH21 53 C3
Merley Ways. BH21 53 C6
Mill La. BH21 53 B4
Mill Stream Clo. BH21 53 B4
Milton Rd. BH21 53 B3
Minster Vw. BH21 53 C3
New Borough Rd. BH21 53 C5
Oakdene Clo. BH21 53 D4
Oakley Hill. BH21 53 C6
Oakley Rd. BH21 53 C6
Old Highway Mews. BH21 53 D4
Old Manor Clo. BH21 53 D4
Old Rd. BH21 53 A4
Onslow Gdns. BH21 53 C3
Osborne Rd. BH21 53 C5
Park La. BH21 53 B4
Parkwood Rd. BH21 53 C4
Pine Tree Clo. BH21 53 D4
Poole Rd. BH21 53 C5
Poplar Clo. BH21 53 C4
Priors Walk. BH21 53 B4
Quince La. BH21 53 D3
Redcotts La. BH21 53 B4
Redcotts Rd. BH21 53 A4
Retreat Rd. BH21 53 C4
Richmond Rd. BH21 53 C5
River Clo. BH21 53 B3
Rodway. BH21 53 C5
Rowlands Hill. BH21 53 C4
Royston Dri. BH21 53 C4
St Catherines. BH21 53 C5
St Johns Hill. BH21 53 C4
St Margarets Clo. BH21 53 A3
St Margarets Hill. BH21 53 A3
School La. BH21 53 B3
Shakespeare Rd. BH21 53 B3
Sheppards Field. BH21 53 B3
Smugglers La. BH21 53 D1
Station Rd. BH21 53 C5
Station Ter. BH21 53 C5
Stevenson Clo. BH21 53 C5
Stone La. BH21 53 A3
Tapper Ct. BH21 53 D5
Tennyson Rd. BH21 53 B3
The Square. BH21 53 B4
Tower La. BH21 53 D3
Trumpeters Ct. BH21 53 B4
Ullswater Rd. BH21 53 C6
Venator Pl. BH21 53 C3
Victoria Pl. BH21 53 A4
Victoria Rd. BH21 53 A4
Walford Clo. BH21 53 B2
Walford Gdns. BH21 53 B3
Welland Rd. BH21 53 C4
Wesley Rd. BH21 53 D3
West Borough. BH21 53 B3
West Row. BH21 53 B4
West St. BH21 53 B4
Westfield Clo. BH21 53 A4
Whitehouse Rd. BH21 53 C6
Whiteways. BH21 53 D3
Willett Rd. BH21 53 A6
Wimborne By-Pass. BH21 53 A6
Wimborne Rd, Colehill. BH21 53 D3
Wimborne Rd, Knobcrook. BH21 53 B3
Yew Tree Clo. BH21 53 C

WOOL

Baileys Dri. BH20 54 B
Bindon La. BH20 54 D
Bindon Way. BH20 54 D
Breachfield. BH20 54 C
Burton Clo. BH20 54 B
Burton La. BH20 54 A
Burton Wood. BH20 54 B
Cedar Clo. BH20 54 C
Chalk Pit La. BH20 54 B
Church La. BH20 54 D
Colliers La. BH20 54 C
Cottage Clo. BH20 54 C
Dorchester Rd. BH20 54 A
Duck St. BH20 54 D
East Burton Rd. BH20 54 A
Fairfields. BH20 54 D
Folly La. BH20 54 C
Frome Av. BH20 54 B
Giddy Green La. BH20 54 A
Giddy Green Rd. BH20 54 A
High St. BH20 54 D
High Street Clo. BH20 54 D
Hillside Rd. BH20 54 C
Hyde Rd. BH20 54 C
Hyde Way. BH20 54 C
Jeremy Clo. BH20 54 D
Knowle Hill. BH20 54 C
Knowlewood Knap. BH20 54 C
Lampton Clo. BH20 54 B
Linclieth Rd. BH20 54 C
Lower Hillside Rd. BH20 54 C
Lulworth Rd. BH20 54 D
Meadow La. BH20 54 C
Moreton Rd. BH20 54 A
New Buildings Rd. BH20 54 A
New Rd. BH20 54 C
Oakdene Rd. BH20 54 B
Quarr Hill. BH20 54 D
Sandhills Cres. BH20 54 A
Spring St. BH20 54 D
Station Rd. BH20 54 C
Sydenham Cres. BH20 54 B
The Alisons. BH20 54 A
The Cross. BH20 54 D
The Square. BH20 54 C
Vicarage Clo. BH20 54 C
Wareham Rd. BH20 54 C
Water Meadow La. BH20 54 A

Edition 136G 7.97